HOT & SPICY

PUBLICATIONS INTERNATIONAL, LTD.

Copyright © by Publications International, Ltd.
All rights reserved. This publication may not be reproduced or quoted in whole or in part by mimeograph or any other printed or electronic means, or for presentation on radio, television, videotape or film without written permission from:

Louis Weber, C.E.O.
Publications International, Ltd.
7373 N. Cicero Ave.
Lincolnwood, IL 60646

Permission is never granted for commercial purposes.

Favorite All Time Recipes is a trademark of Publications International, Ltd.

All recipes and photographs that contain specific brand names are copyrighted by those companies and/or associations, unless otherwise specified. Photographs on pages 11, 14, 16, 18, 20, 22, 24, 48, 51, 63, 67, 68, 71, 75, 77, 82, 88 and 89 copyright © Publications International, Ltd.

Some of the products listed in this publication may be in limited distribution.

Front cover photography by Photo/Kevin Smith, Chicago.

Pictured on the front cover *(clockwise from top left):* Classic Salsa *(page 50),* Deluxe Fajita Nachos *(page 60),* Tomatillo Salsa *(page 50),* Sausage Ham Jambalaya *(page 38)* and Hot, Spicy, Tangy, Sticky Chicken *(page 66).*

Pictured on the back cover *(clockwise from top):* Hoisin Chicken *(page 16),* Aztec Chili Salad *(page 78)* and Smoke-Cooked Beef Ribs *(page 76).*

ISBN: 0-7853-1769-4

Manufactured in U.S.A.

8 7 6 5 4 3 2 1

Microwave Cooking: Microwave ovens vary in wattage. The microwave cooking times given in this publication are approximate. Use the cooking times as guidelines and check for doneness before adding more time. Consult manufacturer's instructions for suitable microwave-safe cooking dishes.

Asian Flare	**6**
Blazing Bayou	**24**
South-of-the-Border Sizzlers	**44**
Hot Off the Grill	**62**
Fire Alarm Chilis	**78**
Acknowledgments	**92**
Index	**93**

ASIAN FLARE

Chicken Curry Bombay

- 1 medium onion, cut into wedges
- 2 cloves garlic, minced
- 2 teaspoons curry powder
- 1 tablespoon olive oil
- 2 half boneless chicken breasts, skinned and sliced ¼ inch thick
- 1 can (14½ ounces) DEL MONTE® Original Recipe Stewed Tomatoes
- ⅓ cup DEL MONTE® Seedless Raisins
- 1 can (16 ounces) DEL MONTE® Whole New Potatoes, drained and cut into chunks
- 1 can (14½ ounces) DEL MONTE® Cut Green Beans, drained

In large skillet, cook onion, garlic and curry in oil until tender, stirring occasionally. Stir in chicken, tomatoes and raisins; bring to boil. Cover and simmer over medium heat 8 minutes. Add potatoes and green beans. Cook, uncovered, 5 minutes, stirring occasionally. Season with salt and pepper, if desired.

Makes 4 servings

Prep time: 10 minutes
Cook time: 18 minutes

Chicken Curry Bombay

Spicy Shrimp with Snow Peas

Spicy Shrimp with Snow Peas

- 6 ounces fresh snow peas, trimmed
- 1 medium red bell pepper, cut into ½-inch strips
- ½ cup diagonally sliced green onions
- 1 tablespoon MAZOLA® Corn Oil
- 1 cup Orient Express Stir-Fry Sauce (recipe follows)
- 1 teaspoon crushed red pepper
- 1 pound medium raw shrimp, peeled and deveined
- Rice (optional)

Microwave Directions: In 3-quart microwavable casserole combine snow peas, bell pepper, onions and corn oil. Microwave covered on HIGH (100%) 1 minute. Stir in Stir-Fry Sauce and crushed red pepper. Microwave 2 minutes. Add shrimp. Microwave 6 to 8 minutes or until sauce boils and thickens and shrimp are opaque, stirring twice. If desired, serve with rice.

Makes 4 servings

Orient Express Stir-Fry Sauce

- 2½ cups chicken broth
- ½ cup ARGO® or KINGSFORD'S® Corn Starch
- ½ cup soy sauce
- ½ cup KARO® Light Corn Syrup
- ½ cup dry sherry
- ¼ cup cider vinegar
- 2 cloves garlic, minced or pressed
- 2 teaspoons grated fresh ginger
- ¼ teaspoon ground red pepper

Combine broth, corn starch, soy sauce, corn syrup, sherry, vinegar, garlic, ginger and red pepper in 1½-quart jar with tight fitting lid. Cover and shake well. Store in refrigerator for up to 3 weeks. Shake well before using. *Makes about 4 cups*

Grilled Lobster with Spicy Sauce

- 4 whole live lobsters (1 to 1½ pounds *each*)*
- ¼ cup dry sherry
- 3 tablespoons soy sauce
- 2 to 3 tablespoons sugar
- 2 teaspoons grated fresh ginger *or* ½ teaspoon ground ginger
- 1 teaspoon dried crushed red chili peppers
- 2 cloves garlic, minced
- Butter or margarine

*2 pounds fresh prawns may be substituted for lobster. Leave shells on and thread onto metal skewers. Grill as above, reducing cooking time to 5 minutes.

8 ASIAN FLARE

Bring large kettle of water to boil. Plunge lobsters into water. Return water to boil; cover and simmer 3 minutes or just until lobsters turn pink. Remove lobsters; rinse with cold water and drain. Turn lobsters, undersides up, and cut through inner shell of tails to expose meat.

For spicy sauce, combine remaining ingredients, except butter. Brush lobster shell and meaty undersides with sauce, letting it soak into meat. Grill lobsters, meat side up, on covered grill, over medium-hot KINGSFORD® with Mesquite Charcoal Briquets 13 to 15 minutes, basting often with sauce, until meat turns opaque. When lobsters are cooked, make a deep cut lengthwise in center of lobsters' undersides with a sharp, pointed knife. Spread halves enough to remove stomach (near head) and black line. Crack claw shells with hammer. Serve with melted butter and remaining spicy sauce. *Makes 4 servings*

Fiery Chicken with Noodles

- 2 tablespoons vegetable oil
- 3 pounds frying chicken pieces
- 1¼ cups water, divided
- 1 medium onion, chopped
- ¼ cup KIKKOMAN® Soy Sauce
- 2 cloves garlic, pressed
- 1½ teaspoons paprika
- ½ teaspoon ground cumin
- ¼ teaspoon ground red pepper
- ¼ teaspoon dried oregano, crumbled
- 4 teaspoons cornstarch
- Hot cooked noodles

Heat oil in large skillet over medium heat. Add chicken and brown on all sides. Remove pieces; drain off oil. Add 1 cup water, onion, soy sauce, garlic, paprika, cumin, red pepper and oregano to same skillet; stir to combine. Arrange chicken pieces over mixture; cover pan and simmer 25 minutes. Turn chicken over; simmer, covered, 20 minutes longer, or until tender. Remove chicken; keep warm. Pour pan juices into large measuring cup. Return 2 cups juices to skillet. Combine remaining ¼ cup water and cornstarch; stir into pan. Cook and stir until mixture boils and thickens. Return chicken pieces to skillet; coat with sauce. Serve over noodles. *Makes 4 to 6 servings*

Fiery Chicken with Noodles

ASIAN FLARE 9

Peanut Chicken

- 1 (3-pound) broiler-fryer chicken, cut up
- 2 teaspoons vegetable oil
- 1 can (14½ ounces) DEL MONTE® Original Recipe Stewed Tomatoes, coarsely chopped, undrained
- 3 tablespoons chunky peanut butter
- 2 cloves garlic, crushed
- 1 teaspoon grated gingerroot
- 1 teaspoon soy sauce
- ⅛ to ¼ teaspoon red pepper flakes
- Chopped peanuts and cilantro (optional)

In large skillet, cook chicken in oil about 25 minutes or until no longer pink; drain. Set chicken aside and keep warm. In same skillet, add undrained tomatoes and remaining ingredients. Simmer 3 minutes. Add chicken; cook 2 minutes or until heated through, turning once. Garnish with chopped peanuts and cilantro, if desired.

Makes 4 to 6 servings

Prep time: 3 minutes
Cook time: 30 minutes

Mongolian Lamb

- 1 pound boneless lamb leg or shoulder
- 3 tablespoons KIKKOMAN® Soy Sauce, divided
- 1 tablespoon cornstarch
- 2 cloves garlic, pressed
- ¾ cup water
- 2½ teaspoons cornstarch
- 1 teaspoon sesame seed, toasted
- ½ teaspoon sugar
- ⅛ to ¼ teaspoon crushed red pepper
- 2 tablespoons vegetable oil, divided
- 2 medium carrots, cut diagonally into thin slices
- 1 bunch green onions, cut into 2-inch lengths, separating whites from tops
- Hot cooked rice

Cut lamb across grain into long, thin slices. Combine 1 tablespoon *each* soy sauce and cornstarch with garlic in medium bowl; stir in lamb. Let stand 10 minutes. Meanwhile, combine water, remaining 2 tablespoons soy sauce, 2½ teaspoons cornstarch, sesame seed, sugar and red pepper; set aside. Heat 1 tablespoon oil in hot wok or large skillet over high heat. Add lamb and stir-fry 1 minute; remove. Heat remaining 1 tablespoon oil in same pan. Add carrots and white parts of green onions; stir-fry 2 minutes. Add green onion tops; stir-fry 1 minute. Add lamb and soy sauce mixture. Cook and stir until sauce boils and thickens. Serve immediately with rice.

Makes 6 servings

Mongolian Lamb

Eggplant Szechuan Style

Eggplant Szechuan Style

- 1 pound Oriental eggplants *or* 1 domestic eggplant
- 3 green onions, divided
- 1 tablespoon minced garlic
- 2 teaspoons minced fresh ginger
- 2 teaspoons hot bean sauce
- ½ cup chicken broth
- 1 tablespoon soy sauce
- 1 tablespoon red wine vinegar
- 1½ teaspoons sugar
- 5 tablespoons vegetable oil, divided
- 1 tablespoon water
- 1 teaspoon cornstarch
- 1 teaspoon sesame oil

Cut unpeeled eggplant into ½-inch-thick slices; cut slices into 2×½-inch strips.

Cut 1 onion into thin slices; reserve for garnish. Cut remaining onions into thin slices. Combine onions, garlic, ginger and hot bean sauce in medium bowl. Combine chicken broth, soy sauce, vinegar and sugar in small bowl.

Heat 2 tablespoons vegetable oil in wok or large skillet over medium-high heat. Add ½ of eggplant and cook, stirring often, until soft and moist, about 5 minutes. Remove to colander; drain. Repeat, using 2 more tablespoons vegetable oil and the remaining eggplant.

Heat remaining 1 tablespoon vegetable oil in wok over medium-high heat. Add onion-garlic mixture and stir-fry 30 seconds; return eggplant to wok. Add chicken broth mixture. Bring to a boil and cook, stirring occasionally, until liquid is almost evaporated.

Blend water and cornstarch in small cup; add to wok. Cook and stir until sauce boils and thickens slightly. Stir in sesame oil. Garnish with reserved onion slices.

Makes 4 to 5 servings

Thai Ribs

- ¼ cup creamy peanut butter
- ¼ cup KIKKOMAN® Soy Sauce
- 3 tablespoons vinegar
- 2 tablespoons sugar
- 1½ teaspoons TABASCO® pepper sauce
- 1 large clove garlic, pressed
- 3 to 4 pounds pork spareribs, cut into 2-rib pieces

Measure peanut butter into small bowl; gradually blend in soy sauce and vinegar until mixture is smooth and creamy. Stir in sugar, TABASCO sauce and garlic. Place ribs, meaty-side down, in shallow, foil-lined baking pan. Brush ribs thoroughly with peanut butter mixture. Cover pan tightly with foil; bake in 350°F. oven 1 hour. Discard foil; drain off drippings. Brush ribs with sauce; bake, uncovered, 15 minutes. Turn ribs over and brush with remaining sauce. Bake 15 minutes longer, or until ribs are golden brown and tender. *Makes 4 to 6 servings*

Hot Chicken with Peanuts

- ½ pound boneless chicken breast
- 1 egg white
- 2 tablespoons KIKKOMAN® Soy Sauce, divided
- 4 teaspoons cornstarch, divided
- 2 tablespoons dry sherry
- 1 teaspoon sugar
- 1 cup peanut oil
- ¼ teaspoon crushed red pepper
- ½ cup roasted peanuts
- ½ cup sliced green onions and tops

Cut chicken breast into ¾-inch cubes. Combine egg white, 1 tablespoon soy sauce and 3 teaspoons cornstarch in small bowl; stir in chicken. Cover and refrigerate 1 hour. Meanwhile, blend remaining 1 tablespoon soy sauce and 1 teaspoon cornstarch, sherry and sugar; set aside. Heat oil in wok or large skillet to 375°F. Stir chicken mixture; spoon into hot oil. Stir-fry 1 minute, or until chicken turns white; remove and drain on paper towels. Pour off all but 1 tablespoon oil from pan. Add red pepper and cooked chicken; stir-fry 1 minute. Add soy sauce mixture; cook and stir until chicken pieces are glazed with sauce. Stir in peanuts and green onions. Serve immediately.
Makes 2 servings

Thai Ribs

Bean Threads with Minced Pork

Bean Threads with Minced Pork

    4 ounces bean threads or Chinese rice vermicelli
    3 dried mushrooms
    1 small red or green hot chili pepper
    3 green onions, divided
    2 tablespoons minced fresh ginger
    2 tablespoons hot bean sauce
1½ cups chicken broth
    1 tablespoon soy sauce
    1 tablespoon dry sherry
    2 tablespoons vegetable oil
    6 ounces lean ground pork
    2 cilantro sprigs, for garnish

Place bean threads and dried mushrooms in separate bowls. Cover each with hot water. Let stand 30 minutes; drain. Cut bean threads into 4-inch pieces. Squeeze out excess water from mushrooms. Cut off and discard stems; cut caps into thin slices.

Cut chili pepper in half and scrape out seeds.* Finely mince pepper. Thinly slice 2 onions. Cut remaining onion into 1½-inch slivers and reserve for garnish.

*Wear rubber or plastic gloves when cutting chili peppers. Do not touch eyes or lips when handling.

Combine ginger and hot bean sauce in small bowl. Combine chicken broth, soy sauce and sherry in medium bowl.

Heat oil in wok or large skillet over high heat. Add pork and stir-fry until meat is no longer pink, about 2 minutes. Add chili pepper, sliced onions and ginger-bean sauce mixture. Stir-fry until meat absorbs color from bean sauce, about 1 minute. Add chicken broth mixture, bean threads and mushrooms. Simmer, uncovered, until most of the liquid is absorbed, about 5 minutes. Garnish with onion slivers and cilantro sprigs.

Makes 4 servings

Grilled Rainbow Trout with Asian Flavors

    1 tablespoon grated fresh ginger
    ¼ cup safflower oil
    ⅛ teaspoon crushed red pepper
    1 teaspoon grated lime peel
    2 tablespoons fresh lime juice
    Salt to taste
    4 CLEAR SPRINGS® Brand Idaho Rainbow Trout fillets, butterflied (6 ounces each)

Cook ginger in oil over medium heat just until lightly browned and aromatic. Remove pan from heat; stir in red pepper. When oil mixture cools completely, whisk gradually into small bowl with lime peel and juice; set aside. Heat grill. Brush grill with oil; grill trout flesh-side down 2 minutes. Gently turn trout; grill 2 minutes more or until opaque. Serve immediately with lime-ginger mixture.

Makes 4 servings

Spicy Chicken Wings

- 2 pounds chicken wings (about 10 wings)
- 4 tablespoons KIKKOMAN® Soy Sauce, divided
- 1 tablespoon dry sherry
- 2 tablespoons vegetable oil
- 1 clove garlic, minced
- 1 teaspoon minced fresh ginger root
- ½ cup chicken stock or water
- 2 teaspoons sugar
- ½ teaspoon crushed red pepper
- 1 tablespoon water
- 2 teaspoons cornstarch

Disjoint chicken wings; discard tips (or save for stock). Combine 1 tablespoon soy sauce and sherry in large bowl. Stir in chicken; set aside. Heat oil in hot wok or large skillet over high heat. Add chicken and cook until lightly browned, stirring occasionally. Drain off excess oil. Add garlic and ginger; stir-fry 1 minute. Combine chicken stock, remaining 3 tablespoons soy sauce, sugar and red pepper; pour over chicken. Cover and simmer 15 minutes. Uncover; simmer 5 minutes longer, or until chicken is tender. Blend water and cornstarch; add to pan. Cook and stir until sauce boils and thickens.

Makes 4 appetizer servings

Shanghai Salad

- 3 tablespoons vegetable oil
- 1 teaspoon minced fresh ginger
- 1 clove garlic, minced
- 1½ cups cooked flank steak or other meat, cut into ½-inch strips
- 1½ cups fresh *or* 1 package (6 ounces) frozen snow peas, thawed and drained
- 1 can (8 ounces) sliced water chestnuts, drained
- ½ cup green onions, cut into ½-inch pieces
- 2 tablespoons dry sherry
- 1 tablespoon soy sauce
- ½ teaspoon TABASCO® pepper sauce
- **Shredded lettuce**

Heat oil in large skillet. Add ginger and garlic; cook 1 minute. Add remaining ingredients except lettuce; stir-fry over high heat until heated through. Spoon onto bed of shredded lettuce. Serve hot with additional TABASCO sauce, if desired. *Makes 3 to 4 servings*

Spicy Chicken Wings

Hoisin Chicken

- 1 broiler-fryer chicken (3 to 4 pounds), cut up
- ½ cup *plus* 1 tablespoon cornstarch, divided
- 1 cup water
- 3 tablespoons dry sherry
- 3 tablespoons cider vinegar
- 3 tablespoons hoisin sauce
- 4 teaspoons soy sauce
- 2 teaspoons instant chicken bouillon granules
- Vegetable oil for frying
- 2 teaspoons minced fresh ginger
- 2 medium yellow onions, chopped
- 8 ounces fresh broccoli, cut into 1-inch pieces
- 1 red or green bell pepper, chopped
- 2 cans (4 ounces each) whole button mushrooms, drained
- Hot cooked vermicelli (optional)
- Additional red bell pepper, cut into strips, for garnish

Rinse chicken; set aside. Combine 1 tablespoon cornstarch, water, sherry, vinegar, hoisin sauce, soy sauce and bouillon granules in small bowl; mix well. Set aside.

Place remaining ½ cup cornstarch in large bowl. Add chicken pieces; stir to coat well. Heat oil in large skillet or wok over high heat to 375°F. Add ⅓ of the chicken pieces, one at a time; cook until no longer pink in center, about 5 minutes. Drain chicken pieces on paper towels. Repeat with remaining chicken.

Remove all but 2 tablespoons oil from skillet. Add ginger; stir-fry 1 minute. Add onions; stir-fry 1 minute. Add broccoli, bell pepper and mushrooms; stir-fry 2 minutes. Stir cornstarch mixture; add to skillet. Cook and stir until sauce boils and turns translucent. Return chicken to skillet. Cook and stir until chicken is thoroughly heated, about 2 minutes. Serve over hot vermicelli and garnish with bell pepper strips, if desired. *Makes 6 servings*

Spicy Grilled Pork Chops

- ¼ cup minced onion
- ¼ cup soy sauce
- 2 tablespoons fresh lime juice
- 2 cloves garlic, minced
- ½ teaspoon crushed red pepper flakes
- 4 center-cut well trimmed pork loin or rib chops, cut ¾ inch thick

Combine onion, soy sauce, lime juice, garlic and crushed red pepper in large plastic bag; add chops. Close bag securely; turn to coat. Marinate in refrigerator at least 4 hours or up to 24 hours, turning once.

Drain chops; reserve marinade. Brush with some reserved marinade. Grill or broil chops 5 to 6 inches from heat 7 minutes. Turn chops over; brush with marinade, discarding remaining marinade. Grill or broil 8 to 13 minutes or until barely pink in center. *Makes 4 servings*

Hoisin Chicken

ASIAN FLARE 19

Two-Onion Pork Shreds

Two-Onion Pork Shreds

- ½ teaspoon Szechuan peppercorns*
- 1 teaspoon cornstarch
- 4 teaspoons soy sauce, divided
- 4 teaspoons dry sherry, divided
- 7½ teaspoons vegetable oil, divided
- 8 ounces boneless lean pork
- 2 teaspoons red wine vinegar
- ½ teaspoon sugar
- 2 cloves garlic, minced
- ½ small yellow onion, cut into ¼-inch slices
- 8 green onions with tops, cut into 2-inch pieces
- ½ teaspoon sesame oil

*Szechuan peppercorns are deceptively potent. Wear rubber or plastic gloves when crushing them and do not touch your eyes or lips when handling.

For marinade, place peppercorns in small skillet. Cook over medium-low heat, shaking skillet frequently, until fragrant, about 2 minutes. Cool. Crush peppercorns with mortar and pestle. Transfer peppercorns to medium bowl. Add cornstarch, 2 teaspoons soy sauce, 2 teaspoons sherry and 1½ teaspoons vegetable oil; mix well. Slice meat ⅛ inch thick; cut into 2×½-inch pieces. Add to marinade; stir to coat well. Let stand 30 minutes.

Combine remaining 2 teaspoons soy sauce, 2 teaspoons sherry, vinegar and sugar in small bowl; mix well. Heat remaining 6 teaspoons vegetable oil in wok or large skillet over high heat. Stir in garlic. Add meat; stir-fry until no longer pink, about 2 minutes. Add yellow onion; stir-fry 1 minute. Add green onions; stir-fry 30 seconds. Add soy-vinegar mixture; cook and stir 30 seconds. Stir in sesame oil.

Makes 2 to 3 servings

Tandoori Chicken

- **4 chicken legs, thighs and drumsticks attached (about 2¼ pounds)***
- 1 tablespoon lemon juice
- 1 teaspoon yellow food coloring
- ½ teaspoon red food coloring
- 1½ tablespoons ground coriander
- 1 tablespoon paprika
- 1 tablespoon ground cumin
- 2 teaspoons salt
- 1¼ cups plain yogurt
- 1 tablespoon grated fresh ginger
- 1 teaspoon garlic, crushed
- ¼ cup melted butter or vegetable oil
- **Lemon wedges**

*Tandoori Chicken can be made with chicken breasts in place of legs; reduce cooking time to about 10 minutes per side.

Remove skin and excess fat from chicken; discard. Mix lemon juice and yellow and red food coloring in cup. Brush chicken with mixture to coat.

Mix coriander, paprika, cumin and salt in cup. Sprinkle mixture over chicken in shallow glass bowl or casserole, turning chicken and spreading spices to evenly coat. Mix yogurt, ginger and garlic in small bowl. Pour yogurt mixture over chicken, turning pieces to coat. Marinate, covered, in refrigerator, turning pieces occasionally, 4 to 6 hours. Let chicken stand in marinade, covered, at room temperature 1 hour before cooking.

Heat oven to 500°F. Remove chicken from bowl, shaking off as much marinade as possible. Place chicken in single layer in greased shallow baking pan; brush chicken with 2 tablespoons melted butter. Bake chicken 12 minutes. Turn pieces over; brush with remaining 2 tablespoons melted butter. Continue baking until chicken is cooked through and tender, about 13 minutes longer. Serve immediately with lemon wedges.   *Makes 4 servings*

Tandoori Chicken

Cantonese-Style Beef and Peppers

Cantonese-Style Beef and Peppers

- ½ pound beef top round or boneless sirloin steak, cut 1 inch thick, or beef flank steak
- ¼ cup water
- 2 tablespoons *each* dry sherry and reduced-sodium soy sauce
- 2 teaspoons cornstarch
- 1½ teaspoons Oriental dark-roasted sesame oil
- 1 teaspoon sugar
- 2 tablespoons peanut, safflower or corn oil, divided
- 1 large red or green bell pepper, cut into ¾-inch chunks
- 1 teaspoon minced fresh ginger
- 1 tablespoon minced green onion

Partially freeze beef top round steak until firm; cut across the grain into ⅛-inch-thick strips. Combine water, sherry, soy sauce, cornstarch, sesame oil and sugar; mix well. Place beef and ⅓ cup sauce mixture in plastic bag or utility dish, turning to coat. Close bag securely or cover dish and marinate in refrigerator 30 minutes, turning at least once. Reserve remaining sauce mixture.

Heat 1 tablespoon peanut oil in large nonstick skillet or wok over medium-high heat until hot. Remove beef from marinade; discard marinade. Stir-fry beef about 1½ minutes or until no longer pink. Remove beef from pan; reserve. Add remaining 1 tablespoon peanut oil to pan; heat until hot. Add pepper and ginger; stir-fry over medium-high heat 2 to 3 minutes or until pepper is crisp-tender. Add reserved sauce mixture, stirring until slightly thickened. Add reserved beef; toss lightly to coat. Sprinkle with onion and serve immediately. *Makes 2 servings*

Freezing time: 30 to 45 minutes
Preparation time: 25 minutes
Cooking time: 9 to 10 minutes

Favorite recipe from **National Cattlemen's Beef Association**

ASIAN FLARE

Two-Onion Pork Shreds

Two-Onion Pork Shreds

- ½ teaspoon Szechuan peppercorns*
- 1 teaspoon cornstarch
- 4 teaspoons soy sauce, divided
- 4 teaspoons dry sherry, divided
- 7½ teaspoons vegetable oil, divided
- 8 ounces boneless lean pork
- 2 teaspoons red wine vinegar
- ½ teaspoon sugar
- 2 cloves garlic, minced
- ½ small yellow onion, cut into ¼-inch slices
- 8 green onions with tops, cut into 2-inch pieces
- ½ teaspoon sesame oil

*Szechuan peppercorns are deceptively potent. Wear rubber or plastic gloves when crushing them and do not touch your eyes or lips when handling.

For marinade, place peppercorns in small skillet. Cook over medium-low heat, shaking skillet frequently, until fragrant, about 2 minutes. Cool. Crush peppercorns with mortar and pestle. Transfer peppercorns to medium bowl. Add cornstarch, 2 teaspoons soy sauce, 2 teaspoons sherry and 1½ teaspoons vegetable oil; mix well. Slice meat ⅛ inch thick; cut into 2×½-inch pieces. Add to marinade; stir to coat well. Let stand 30 minutes.

Combine remaining 2 teaspoons soy sauce, 2 teaspoons sherry, vinegar and sugar in small bowl; mix well. Heat remaining 6 teaspoons vegetable oil in wok or large skillet over high heat. Stir in garlic. Add meat; stir-fry until no longer pink, about 2 minutes. Add yellow onion; stir-fry 1 minute. Add green onions; stir-fry 30 seconds. Add soy-vinegar mixture; cook and stir 30 seconds. Stir in sesame oil.

Makes 2 to 3 servings

Thai Chicken Curry

- 1 can (14½ ounces) DEL MONTE® Original Recipe Stewed Tomatoes
- 2 teaspoons curry powder
- 1 teaspoon sugar
- ½ teaspoon grated lemon peel
- ¼ to ½ teaspoon minced jalapeño chile
- 1 pound boneless, skinless chicken, cut into ¾-inch cubes
- ¾ cup coconut milk*
- 3 tablespoons thinly sliced fresh basil leaves *or* 1 teaspoon dried basil
- Hot cooked rice

*If coconut milk is not available, omit sugar. Add 3 tablespoons shredded coconut to tomatoes. Substitute ½ cup whipping cream for coconut milk; add after chicken is done. Cook, uncovered, over low heat until heated through.

In large skillet, combine tomatoes, curry, sugar, lemon peel and jalapeño. Cook, uncovered, over medium-high heat 7 minutes or until thickened, stirring occasionally. Season chicken with salt and pepper, if desired. Add chicken, coconut milk and basil to skillet. Cover; cook over medium heat 8 minutes or until chicken is no longer pink. Serve over hot cooked rice.

Makes 3 to 4 servings

Prep & Cook time: 25 minutes

Spicy-Sweet Pineapple Pork

- 1 pound pork loin, cut into ½-inch strips or cubes
- ¾ cup LAWRY'S® Fajitas Skillet Sauce
- 1 tablespoon finely chopped fresh ginger
- 2 tablespoons vegetable oil, divided
- 1 green bell pepper, cut into chunks
- 3 green onions, diagonally sliced into 1-inch pieces
- 1 cup hot salsa
- 3 tablespoons brown sugar
- 2 tablespoons cornstarch
- 2 cans (8 ounces *each*) pineapple chunks in juice, divided
- ½ cup whole cashews

Place pork in large resealable plastic bag. Combine Fajitas Skillet Sauce and ginger; add to pork and marinate in refrigerator 1 hour. In large skillet or wok, heat 1 tablespoon oil. Add bell pepper and onions and stir-fry 3 minutes; remove and set aside. Add pork and remaining 1 tablespoon oil to skillet; stir-fry 5 minutes or until just browned. Return bell pepper and green onions to skillet. In small bowl, combine salsa, brown sugar, cornstarch and juice from one can pineapple. Add to skillet; cook until thickened, stirring constantly. Drain remaining can pineapple. Add all pineapple chunks and cashews; simmer 5 minutes.

Makes 6 servings

Kung Pao Chicken

- 3½ teaspoons cornstarch, divided
- 5 teaspoons soy sauce, divided
- 5 teaspoons dry sherry, divided
- ¼ teaspoon salt
- 3 boneless skinless chicken breast halves, cut into bite-size pieces
- 1 tablespoon red wine vinegar
- 2 tablespoons chicken broth *or* water
- 1½ teaspoons sugar
- 3 tablespoons vegetable oil, divided
- ⅓ cup salted peanuts
- 6 to 8 small dried hot chili peppers
- 1½ teaspoons minced fresh ginger
- 2 green onions with tops, cut into 1½-inch pieces
- Green onion and additional dried hot chili pepper, for garnish

For marinade, combine 2 teaspoons cornstarch, 2 teaspoons soy sauce, 2 teaspoons sherry and salt in large bowl; mix well. Add chicken; stir to coat well. Let stand 30 minutes.

Combine remaining 1½ teaspoons cornstarch, 3 teaspoons soy sauce, 3 teaspoons sherry, vinegar, chicken broth and sugar in small bowl; mix well. Set aside. Heat 1 tablespoon oil in wok or large skillet over medium heat. Add peanuts; cook and stir until lightly toasted. Remove peanuts from wok; set aside. Heat remaining 2 tablespoons oil in wok over medium heat. Add chili peppers; stir-fry until peppers just begin to char, about 1 minute. Increase heat to high. Add chicken mixture; stir-fry 2 minutes. Add ginger; stir-fry until chicken is no longer pink in center, about 1 minute. Add peanuts and onions. Stir cornstarch mixture; add to wok. Cook and stir until sauce boils and thickens. Garnish with onion and chili pepper, if desired.

Makes 3 servings

Sweet 'n Spicy Ribs

- ¼ cup butter or margarine
- 1 medium onion, coarsely chopped
- 1 cup (8 ounces) WISH-BONE® Sweet 'n Spicy French Dressing
- ⅓ cup brown sugar
- 2 tablespoons chili powder
- 1 tablespoon ground cumin
- 1 tablespoon Worcestershire sauce
- ¼ teaspoon hot pepper sauce
- 5 pounds spareribs, baby back or country-style ribs

Preheat oven to 375°F.

In large saucepan, melt butter and cook onion over medium-high heat, stirring frequently, 5 minutes or until tender. Stir in Sweet 'n Spicy French Dressing, brown sugar, chili powder, cumin, Worcestershire sauce and hot pepper sauce.

Meanwhile, in large aluminum foil-lined baking pan or on broiler rack, arrange spareribs, meaty side up, and bake 20 minutes. Brush spareribs generously with sauce; continue baking, meaty side up, brushing occasionally with remaining sauce, 50 minutes or until spareribs are done.

Makes about 7 servings

Kung Pao Chicken

BLAZING BAYOU

Seafood Gumbo

- 1 bag SUCCESS® Rice
- 1 tablespoon reduced-calorie margarine
- ¼ cup chopped onion
- ¼ cup chopped green bell pepper
- 2 cloves garlic, minced
- 1 can (28 ounces) whole tomatoes, cut up, undrained
- 2 cups chicken broth
- ½ teaspoon ground red pepper
- ½ teaspoon dried thyme leaves, crushed
- ½ teaspoon dried basil leaves, crushed
- ¾ pound white fish, cut into 1-inch pieces
- 1 package (10 ounces) frozen cut okra, thawed and drained
- ½ pound raw shrimp, peeled and deveined

Prepare rice according to package directions.

Melt margarine in large saucepan over medium-high heat. Add onion, bell pepper and garlic; cook and stir until crisp-tender. Stir in tomatoes, broth, red pepper, thyme and basil. Bring to a boil. Reduce heat to low; simmer, uncovered, until thoroughly heated, 10 to 15 minutes. Stir in fish, okra and shrimp; simmer until fish flakes easily with fork and shrimp curl and turn pink. Add rice; heat thoroughly, stirring occasionally, 5 to 8 minutes. *Makes 4 servings*

Chicken, Andouille Smoked Sausage and Tasso Jambalaya

- 3 tablespoons unsalted butter or margarine
- ½ pound tasso or other smoked ham, diced
- ½ pound andouille smoked sausage or other smoked pork sausage such as Polish sausage (kielbasa), cut into ¼-inch slices
- ¾ pound boneless chicken, cut into bite-size pieces
- 2 bay leaves
- 2 tablespoons Chef Paul Prudhomme's POULTRY MAGIC®
- 1 cup chopped onions, divided
- 1 cup chopped celery, divided
- 1 cup chopped green bell pepper, divided
- 1 tablespoon minced garlic
- ½ cup canned tomato sauce
- 1 cup peeled, chopped tomatoes
- 2½ cups chicken stock or water
- 1½ cups uncooked rice (preferably converted)

Melt butter in 4-quart saucepan over high heat. Add tasso and andouille sausage; cook until meat starts to brown, 4 to 5 minutes, stirring frequently and scraping pan bottom well. Add chicken; continue cooking until chicken is brown, 4 to 5 minutes, stirring frequently and scraping pan bottom as needed. Stir in bay leaves, Poultry Magic® and ½ cup *each* of onions, celery and bell pepper; add garlic. Cook until vegetables are tender, about 6 to 8 minutes, stirring and scraping pan bottom frequently. Stir in tomato sauce and cook about 1 minute, stirring often. Stir in remaining onions, celery, bell pepper and tomatoes. Stir in stock and rice; mix well. Bring mixture to a boil, stirring occasionally. Reduce heat and simmer, covered, over very low heat until rice is tender but still chewy, about 30 minutes. (If you prefer to finish this dish by baking it once stock and rice are added, transfer mixture to an ungreased 13×9-inch baking pan and bake, uncovered, at 350°F until rice is tender but still chewy, about 1 hour.) Stir well; remove bay leaves. Let sit, uncovered, 5 minutes before serving.

To serve, arrange 2 heaping ½-cup mounds of rice on each serving plate for main dish; allow heaping ½ cup for an appetizer.
Makes 6 main-dish servings or 12 appetizer servings

Chicken, Andouille Smoked Sausage and Tasso Jambalaya

Shrimp Creole

Shrimp Creole

- 3½ pounds large shrimp, with shells and heads
- 2½ cups shrimp stock
- ¼ cup vegetable oil
- 2½ cups finely chopped onions, divided
- 1¾ cups finely chopped celery
- 1½ cups finely chopped green bell peppers
- 4 tablespoons unsalted butter or margarine, divided
- 2 teaspoons minced garlic
- 1 bay leaf
- 2 tablespoons Chef Paul Prudhomme's SEAFOOD MAGIC®
- 1½ teaspoons Chef Paul Prudhomme's MAGIC PEPPER SAUCE®
- 3 cups peeled, finely chopped tomatoes (preferably Creole)
- 1½ cups tomato sauce
- 2 teaspoons sugar
- 5 cups hot cooked rice (preferably converted)

Rinse and peel shrimp; make stock from shells and heads.

Heat oil over high heat in 4-quart saucepan. Add 1 cup onions; cook over high heat about 3 minutes, stirring frequently. Reduce heat to medium-low and continue cooking, stirring frequently, 3 to 5 minutes, or until onions turn rich brown. Add remaining onions, celery, bell peppers and 2 tablespoons butter. Cook over high heat until bell peppers and celery are tender, stirring occasionally. Add garlic, bay leaf and Seafood Magic®; stir well. Add Magic Pepper Sauce® and ½ cup stock. Cook over medium heat about 5 minutes for seasonings to blend and vegetables to brown, stirring occasionally, scraping pan bottom. Add tomatoes; reduce heat to low and simmer 10 minutes, stirring occasionally, scraping pan bottom. Stir in tomato sauce and simmer 5 minutes, stirring occasionally. Add remaining stock and sugar. Continue simmering 15 minutes, stirring occasionally. Add shrimp and cook just until plump and pink, 3 to 4 minutes.

To serve, center ½ cup mounded rice on each plate; spoon 1 cup sauce around the rice and arrange 8 or 9 shrimp on top.

Makes 10 servings

Louisiana Barbecue Ribs

- 2 to 2½ pounds country-style ribs or baby back loin ribs
- 3 tablespoons Chef Paul Prudhomme's PORK AND VEAL MAGIC®, divided
- ½ pound sliced bacon, minced
- 1½ cups chopped onions
- About 3 cups pork, beef or chicken stock *or* water
- 1½ cups chili sauce
- 1¼ cups honey
- ¾ cup coarsely chopped dry roasted pecans
- 5 tablespoons freshly squeezed orange juice (slice and save peel and pulp from ½ the orange)
- 2 tablespoons freshly squeezed lemon juice (slice and save peel and pulp from ¼ the lemon)
- 2 teaspoons minced garlic
- 1 teaspoon Chef Paul Prudhomme's MAGIC PEPPER SAUCE®
- 4 tablespoons unsalted butter

Adjust rack about 6 inches from heat source; preheat broiler. If using loin ribs, cut ribs into 2-rib pieces. Place ribs in roasting pan in single layer and sprinkle generously and evenly on both sides with Pork and Veal Magic® (use a total of about 1 tablespoon), pressing it in with your fingers. Broil ribs until well browned on all sides, about 15 minutes, turning as needed. Reserve in roasting pan.

Meanwhile, in 2-quart saucepan, fry bacon over high heat until crisp. Stir in onions; cover pan and cook until onions are dark brown but not burned, 8 to 10 minutes, stirring often. Stir in remaining Pork and Veal Magic®; cook about 1 minute more, stirring often. Remove from heat and reserve.

Place 3 cups stock in 4-quart saucepan; cover. Bring stock to a boil over high heat. Add reserved broiled ribs to stock (set aside roasting pan with drippings still in it). Re-cover saucepan; cook 10 minutes, stirring occasionally. Remove pan from heat and ladle 2 cups stock into roasting pan with drippings. Set aside saucepan containing ribs and remaining stock. Stir drippings in roasting pan well to dissolve all browned bits; reserve.

Return saucepan with bacon-onion mixture to high heat. Stir in chili sauce, honey, pecans, orange juice, lemon juice, orange and lemon peels and pulp, garlic and Magic Pepper Sauce®, stirring well. Add stock-drippings mixture from roasting pan to bacon mixture and bring to a boil; reduce heat to low. Remove orange and lemon peels. Cook, stirring, about 15 minutes more to let flavors blend. Add butter and stir until melted; remove from heat. Pour mixture in batches into blender or food processor fitted with metal blade; process just until pecans and bacon are finely chopped, 10 to 20 seconds. Add processed sauce to saucepan containing ribs. Increase heat to high and bring to a boil. Reduce heat to very low and simmer 10 minutes, stirring occasionally. If ribs are not tender, add additional stock; cook until fork-tender.

Makes 4 servings

Louisiana Pork Chops

- 1 teaspoon garlic powder
- ¼ teaspoon black pepper
- ¼ teaspoon white pepper
- ¼ teaspoon cayenne pepper
- 4 pork chops, ¾ inch thick
- 1 tablespoon butter or margarine
- 1 can (14½ ounces) DEL MONTE® Cajun Recipe Stewed Tomatoes

Combine garlic powder and peppers. Sprinkle on both sides of meat. In large skillet, heat butter over medium-high heat. Add meat; cook 5 minutes. Turn over and cook 4 minutes; drain. Add tomatoes. Cover and cook over medium heat 10 minutes or until meat is cooked. Remove meat to serving dish; keep warm. Cook sauce until thickened; spoon over meat.

Makes 4 servings

Prep time: 5 minutes
Cook time: 21 minutes

Shrimp Gumbo

- 1 package (16 ounces) frozen cut okra
- 1 can (16 ounces) stewed tomatoes, undrained
- 2 cups water
- ½ pound cooked ham or sausage, diced
- 1 can (8 ounces) tomato sauce
- 2 medium onions, sliced
- 2 tablespoons vegetable oil
- ½ teaspoon crushed red pepper flakes
- 1 bay leaf
  Salt and pepper
- 2 pounds shelled deveined raw shrimp

Combine all ingredients except shrimp in Dutch oven. Bring to a boil over high heat. Reduce heat to low. Simmer, partially covered, 30 minutes. Add shrimp; stir well. Cook, partially covered, stirring occasionally, until shrimp are cooked through, 10 to 15 minutes longer. Remove bay leaf before serving.

Makes 6 servings

Creole Chicken Jambalaya

- ¼ cup vegetable oil
- 2 medium onions, chopped
- 6 green onions, chopped
- 2 medium green bell peppers, chopped
- 1 (2½- to 3-pound) broiler-fryer chicken, cut into 8 pieces
- ½ pound cooked ham, cubed
- ½ pound smoked sausage or Polish sausage, cut into ½-inch slices
- 1 can (16 ounces) tomatoes, cut into pieces, undrained
- 1 can (6 ounces) tomato paste
- 1 teaspoon salt
- 1¾ cups uncooked rice
- ½ cup water
- ¾ teaspoon TABASCO® pepper sauce

In large saucepan or Dutch oven heat oil. Add onions, green onions and peppers; cook 10 minutes or until tender. Add chicken; brown on all sides, about 10 minutes. Add ham, sausage, tomatoes with juice, tomato paste and salt. Cover; simmer 10 minutes; stir in rice. Add water. Cover; simmer 1 hour or until chicken is no longer pink in center, stirring frequently. Add additional water if rice begins to stick to bottom of pan. Before serving, stir in TABASCO sauce.

Makes 8 servings

Louisiana Pork Chop

Shrimp Etoufée

- ½ cup butter or margarine
- 2 medium onions, chopped
- 1 cup chopped celery
- 1 cup chopped green onions
- 2 cloves garlic, minced
- ½ cup all-purpose flour
- 4 cups water
- 2 cans (16 ounces each) tomatoes, drained
- 2 tablespoons lemon juice
- 1 teaspoon salt
- 2 bay leaves
- ¼ teaspoon dried thyme leaves
- 2 pounds raw shrimp, peeled, deveined
- ½ teaspoon TABASCO® pepper sauce
- Hot cooked rice

Melt butter in large saucepan or Dutch oven; add onions, celery, green onions and garlic. Cook 5 minutes or until tender. Add flour; stir until well blended. Stir in water, tomatoes, lemon juice, salt, bay leaves and thyme. Bring to a boil, reduce heat and simmer covered 30 minutes; stir occasionally. Add shrimp and TABASCO sauce. Simmer 5 minutes longer or until shrimp turn pink. Remove bay leaves. Serve over rice.

Makes 8 servings

Jambalaya

- 1 bag SUCCESS® Rice
- 1 tablespoon olive oil
- 1 cup sliced turkey sausage
- ½ cup chopped celery
- ½ cup chopped green bell pepper
- ½ cup chopped red bell pepper
- ½ cup chopped red onion
- 1 teaspoon garlic powder
- ¼ teaspoon black pepper
- ¼ teaspoon ground red pepper

Prepare rice according to package directions.

Heat oil in large skillet. Add all remaining ingredients except rice; cook and stir until vegetables are crisp-tender, 5 to 10 minutes. Add rice; heat thoroughly, stirring occasionally. *Makes 4 servings*

Cajun Chicken

- 2½ pounds chicken pieces, skinned (breasts, thighs, legs)
- 1 tablespoon vegetable oil
- 2 cloves garlic, crushed
- ½ teaspoon dried thyme
- 1 can (14½ ounces) DEL MONTE® Cajun Recipe Stewed Tomatoes
- 1 red or green bell pepper, cut into strips
- 1 stalk celery, sliced
- 1 carrot, thinly sliced
- Sliced green onions (optional)

In large skillet, brown chicken in oil over medium-high heat, 10 to 15 minutes; drain. Season with salt and pepper, if desired. Stir garlic and thyme into tomatoes; pour over chicken. Add bell pepper strips, celery and carrot. Bring to boil; cover and simmer 15 minutes or until chicken is no longer pink. Garnish with sliced onions, if desired.

Makes 4 to 6 servings

Prep time: 8 minutes
Cook time: 30 minutes

Sausage-Chicken Creole

- 1 can (14½ ounces) whole tomatoes, undrained and cut up
- ½ cup uncooked rice
- ½ cup hot water
- 2 teaspoons FRANK'S® Original RedHot® Cayenne Pepper Sauce
- ¼ teaspoon garlic powder
- ¼ teaspoon dried oregano, crumbled
- 1 bag (16 ounces) frozen vegetable combination (broccoli, corn, red pepper), thawed and drained
- 1 can (2.8 ounces) FRENCH'S® French Fried Onions
- 4 chicken thighs, skinned
- ½ pound link Italian sausage, quartered and cooked*
- 1 can (8 ounces) tomato sauce

*To cook sausage, simmer in water to cover until done. Or, place in microwave-safe dish and cook, covered, on HIGH 3 minutes or until done.

Preheat oven to 375°F. In 8×12-inch baking dish, combine tomatoes with juice, uncooked rice, hot water, cayenne pepper sauce and seasonings. Bake, covered, at 375° for 10 minutes. Stir vegetables and ½ can French Fried Onions into rice mixture; top with chicken and cooked sausage. Pour tomato sauce over chicken and sausage. Bake, covered, at 375° for 40 minutes or until chicken is done. Top chicken with remaining onions; bake, uncovered, 3 minutes or until onions are golden brown.

Makes 4 servings

Sausage-Chicken Creole

Flaky Southern Biscuits

- 2 cups flour
- 1 tablespoon baking powder
- ½ teaspoon salt
- ½ cup chilled vegetable shortening
- ¾ cup cold milk

Preheat oven to 425°F. In large bowl combine flour, baking powder and salt. With pastry blender or 2 knives used scissors-fashion, cut in shortening until mixture resembles coarse crumbs. Stir in milk just until dough holds together. On lightly floured board knead gently about 1 minute. With floured rolling pin roll dough ½ inch thick. With floured biscuit cutter, cut dough into 2½- to 3-inch rounds. Place 1 inch apart on ungreased cookie sheet. Bake 12 to 15 minutes or until lightly browned. Serve hot.   *Makes 10 biscuits*

BLAZING BAYOU

Cajun-Style Chicken Nuggets

- 1 envelope LIPTON® Recipe Secrets® Onion Soup Mix
- ½ cup plain dry bread crumbs
- 1½ teaspoons chili powder
- 1 teaspoon ground cumin
- 1 teaspoon thyme leaves (optional)
- ¼ teaspoon ground red pepper
- 2 pounds boneless chicken breasts, cut into 1-inch pieces
- Vegetable oil
- Assorted mustards (optional)

In large bowl, combine Onion Soup Mix, bread crumbs, chili powder, cumin, thyme and pepper. Dip chicken in bread crumb mixture, coating well.

In large skillet, heat ½ inch oil and cook chicken over medium heat, turning once, until done; drain on paper towels. Serve warm and, if desired, with assorted mustards.

Makes about 5 dozen nuggets

Steak Etouffée

- 1 tablespoon *plus* 2 teaspoons Chef Paul Prudhomme's MEAT MAGIC®
- About 2 pounds beef round steak, cut into 4 pieces
- ¼ cup vegetable oil
- ¼ cup all-purpose flour
- 3 cups julienned onions
- 1 tablespoon margarine
- ¼ cup white vinegar
- 3 cups beef stock or water, divided

Sprinkle Meat Magic® evenly over both sides of steak pieces; reserve.

Heat oil in 8-quart heavy saucepan over high heat, 2½ to 3 minutes or until oil just starts to smoke. Coat seasoned meat with flour and cook, in a single layer, in hot oil. Cook about 5 minutes or until meat is browned. Turn meat pieces over and cook 3 to 4 minutes or until browned. Remove with a slotted spoon and reserve.

In same saucepan, add onions and margarine; stir and scrape sides and bottom of pan well to get up all browned bits. Cook, stirring frequently, about 4 minutes; add vinegar, stirring and scraping once more. Cook, stirring and scraping pan bottom well, about 3 minutes. Stir in 1 cup stock; cook, stirring occasionally, about 2 minutes. Stir in 1 cup more stock; cook, stirring occasionally, about 5 minutes. Stir in remaining stock and return browned meat to pan. Bring mixture to a boil, cover and reduce heat to simmer. Cook, stirring occasionally, about 1½ hours or until gravy has thickened slightly and meat is fork-tender.

Makes 4 servings

Spicy Crab Soup

- 1 pound crabmeat,* cooked, flaked and cartilage removed
- 1 can (28 ounces) crushed tomatoes in tomato purée, undrained
- 2 cups water
- 1 can (10¾ ounces) low-sodium chicken broth
- ¾ cup chopped celery
- ¾ cup diced onion
- 1 teaspoon seafood seasoning
- ¼ teaspoon lemon-pepper
- 1 package (10 ounces) frozen corn, thawed
- 1 package (10 ounces) frozen peas, thawed

*Purchase flake-style or a mixture of flake and chunk crabmeat if purchasing blue crab or surimi blended seafood.

Combine tomatoes with purée, water, broth, celery, onion, seafood seasoning and lemon-pepper in 6-quart saucepan. Bring to a boil over high heat. Reduce heat to low. Cover and simmer 20 to 30 minutes. Add corn and peas; simmer 10 minutes more. Add crabmeat; simmer until heated through.

Makes 6 servings

Favorite recipe from National Fisheries Institute

Bayou Dirty Rice

- ¼ pound spicy sausage, crumbled
- ½ medium onion, chopped
- 1 stalk celery, sliced
- 1 package (6 ounces) wild and long-grain rice seasoned mix
- 1 can (14½ ounces) DEL MONTE® Cajun Recipe Stewed Tomatoes
- ½ green bell pepper, chopped
- ¼ cup chopped parsley

In large skillet, brown sausage and onion over medium-high heat; drain. Add celery, rice and rice seasoning packet; cook and stir 2 minutes. Drain tomatoes reserving liquid; pour liquid into measuring cup. Add water to measure 1⅓ cups; pour over rice. Add tomatoes; bring to boil. Cover and cook over low heat 20 minutes. Add bell pepper and parsley. Cover and cook 5 minutes or until rice is tender. Serve with roasted chicken or Cornish game hens.

Makes 4 to 6 servings

Prep & Cook time: 40 minutes

Spicy Crab Soup

Seafood Gumbo

- ½ cup chopped onion
- ½ cup chopped green bell pepper
- ½ cup (about 2 ounces) sliced fresh mushrooms
- 1 clove garlic, minced
- 2 tablespoons margarine
- 1 can (28 ounces) whole tomatoes, undrained
- 2 cups chicken broth
- ½ to ¾ teaspoon ground red pepper
- ½ teaspoon dried thyme leaves, crushed
- ½ teaspoon dried basil leaves, crushed
- 1 package (10 ounces) frozen cut okra, thawed
- ¾ pound white fish, cut into 1-inch pieces
- ½ pound peeled, deveined raw shrimp
- 3 cups hot cooked rice

Cook onion, bell pepper, mushrooms, and garlic in margarine in large saucepan or Dutch oven over medium-high heat until crisp-tender. Stir in tomatoes with juice, broth, red pepper, thyme, and basil. Bring to a boil. Reduce heat; simmer, uncovered, 10 to 15 minutes. Stir in okra, fish, and shrimp; simmer until fish flakes easily when tested with fork, 5 to 8 minutes. Serve rice over gumbo. *Makes 6 servings*

Favorite recipe from **USA Rice Council**

Okra-Bacon Casserole

- 1½ pounds young fresh okra
- 3 large tomatoes, chopped
- 1 medium onion, chopped
- 1 small green bell pepper, chopped
- ½ teaspoon TABASCO® pepper sauce
- 5 slices bacon

Preheat oven to 350°F. Slice okra into thin rounds. In greased 2½-quart casserole arrange okra, tomatoes, onion and bell pepper. Season with TABASCO sauce. Place bacon on top. Bake uncovered 1½ hours or until okra is tender.
Makes 6 to 8 servings

Note: Two 10-ounce packages frozen okra, thawed, may be substituted for fresh okra. Bake casserole 1 hour.

Microwave Directions: In 2½-quart microwave-safe casserole place bacon; cover with paper towel. Cook at HIGH (100% power) 4 to 5 minutes or until crisp; remove to paper towel to cool, then crumble and set aside. Place okra, onion and bell pepper into drippings in same casserole; season with TABASCO sauce. Cover loosely with plastic wrap; cook at HIGH (100% power) 15 to 18 minutes or until okra is just tender. Add tomatoes. Re-cover; cook at HIGH (100% power) 1 to 2 minutes or until tomatoes are tender. Sprinkle with reserved bacon before serving.

Seafood Gumbo

Sausage Ham Jambalaya

Sausage Ham Jambalaya

- 6 ounces spicy smoked sausage links, sliced
- 6 ounces cooked ham, diced
- 2 cans (14½ ounces *each*) DEL MONTE® Cajun Recipe Stewed Tomatoes
- 1 cup uncooked long-grain white rice
- 1 large clove garlic, minced
- 1 tablespoon chopped fresh parsley
- 1 bay leaf

In heavy 4-quart saucepan, brown sausage and ham. Drain tomatoes reserving liquid; pour liquid into measuring cup. Add water to measure 1½ cups. Add reserved liquid, tomatoes and remaining ingredients to sausage mixture. Cover and simmer 30 to 35 minutes, stirring occasionally. Remove bay leaf. Garnish with additional chopped parsley, if desired.

Makes 4 to 6 servings

Prep time: 10 minutes
Cook time: 40 minutes

Chicken Creole

- 2 bags SUCCESS® Rice
- 1 cup thinly sliced onion
- 1 cup chopped celery
- 1 cup chopped green bell pepper
- 3 cloves garlic, minced
- 2 cups sliced fresh mushrooms
- 2 cups chopped uncooked chicken
- 1 can (14½ ounces) no-salt-added tomatoes, drained
- ½ cup Chablis or other dry white wine
- ¼ teaspoon red pepper flakes
- 1 bay leaf
- ¼ cup chopped green onions

Prepare rice according to package directions.

Spray large nonstick skillet with cooking spray; place over medium-high heat until hot. Add onion, celery, bell pepper and garlic; cook and stir until crisp-tender. Add mushrooms; cook and stir 3 minutes. Add chicken, tomatoes, wine, red pepper flakes and bay leaf. Reduce heat to low; simmer, stirring occasionally, until chicken is no longer pink in center, about 25 minutes. Remove bay leaf. Serve over hot rice; sprinkle with green onions.

Makes 8 servings

Hot and Spicy Barbecued Shrimp

- 1 pound large raw shrimp, peeled and tails left intact
- 1 cup HUNT'S® All Natural Hot & Spicy Barbecue Sauce
- ½ cup butter, melted
- Garlic powder
- Ground red pepper (optional)

To butterfly shrimp, cut shrimp in half vertically almost all the way through and lay flaps open. In small mixing bowl, combine barbecue sauce and butter until well blended. Lay shrimp, cut side up in 9-inch pan. Sprinkle lightly with garlic powder and red pepper. Pour barbecue sauce mixture over shrimp. Cover and refrigerate 6 hours or overnight. This mixture will thicken and may become hard. Over hot barbecue coals or under preheated broiler, cook shrimp 3 to 4 minutes on each side or to desired doneness. While shrimp cooks, heat *remaining* barbecue sauce mixture until bubbling. Dip cooked shrimp in warm sauce.

Makes 4 servings or approximately 18 appetizers

Chicken Creole

Chicken Smothered in Roasted Garlic with Sweet Basil Red Gravy

    Roasted Garlic (recipe follows)
2 cups vegetable or olive oil
1 chicken (about 3 pounds), cut into 8 pieces
2 tablespoons *plus* **2 teaspoons Chef Paul Prudhomme's POULTRY MAGIC®, divided**
1 cup all-purpose flour
2 cups finely chopped onions
3 bay leaves
1 cup finely chopped green bell peppers
3½ cups peeled, chopped tomatoes
1 cup tomato sauce
3 tablespoons chopped fresh basil *or* **1½ teaspoons dried basil leaves**
2 tablespoons light brown sugar
3 cups chicken stock or water
½ teaspoon salt
    Hot cooked rice (preferably converted) or pasta

Prepare Roasted Garlic; reserve. Heat oil in large skillet over high heat. Season chicken with 1 tablespoon Poultry Magic®. Blend flour and 2 teaspoons Poultry Magic® in another container. Dust chicken pieces with seasoned flour. Add chicken pieces to hot oil (large pieces and skin side down first); brown 3 to 4 minutes on each side. When brown (chicken should not be fully cooked), remove chicken pieces from skillet and drain on paper towels. Pour off all but ¼ cup of oil. Reheat skillet and oil over high heat; add onions. Reduce heat to medium; add 2 teaspoons Poultry Magic® and bay leaves. Cook until onions are brown, stirring occasionally, about 5 minutes. Add bell peppers and cook 2 minutes.

Add tomatoes; increase heat to high and cook 1 minute. Stir in tomato sauce and basil; cook about 1 minute. Add Roasted Garlic; cook about 1 minute. Stir in brown sugar; cook about 3 minutes. Add remaining teaspoon Poultry Magic®; cook about 1 minute, then stir in stock. Return chicken pieces to skillet and bring to a boil. Simmer, uncovered, about 25 minutes, stirring occasionally to keep from sticking. Add salt; cook about 1 minute more. Remove bay leaves before serving. Serve with rice or pasta. *Makes 4 servings*

Roasted Garlic

35 unpeeled garlic cloves
Vegetable oil, if using

Method I: Immerse unpeeled garlic cloves in 350°F oil until outer leaves start to turn brown. Cool naturally and peel.

Method II: Place unpeeled garlic cloves on baking sheet or in shallow baking pan. Do not crowd. Bake in preheated 400°F oven until outer leaves are dry looking and edges start to turn brown, 12 to 15 minutes. Cool naturally and peel.

Chicken Smothered in Roasted Garlic with Sweet Basil Red Gravy

Red Beans and Rice

- ½ cup chopped onion
- ½ cup chopped celery
- ½ cup chopped green bell pepper
- 2 cloves garlic, minced
- 2 cans (15 ounces each) red beans,* drained
- ½ pound fully cooked low fat turkey sausage, cut into ¼-inch slices
- 1 can (8 ounces) tomato sauce
- 1 teaspoon Worcestershire sauce
- ¼ teaspoon ground red pepper
- ¼ teaspoon hot pepper sauce
- 3 cups hot cooked rice
- Hot pepper sauce (optional)

*Substitute your favorite bean for red beans.

Coat Dutch oven with nonstick cooking spray and place over medium-high heat until hot. Add onion, celery, bell pepper and garlic. Cook 2 to 3 minutes. Add beans, sausage, tomato sauce, Worcestershire sauce, red pepper, and pepper sauce. Reduce heat; cover and simmer 15 minutes. Serve beans with rice and pepper sauce.

Makes 6 servings

Favorite recipe from **USA Rice Council**

Louisiana Shrimp and Chicken Gumbo

- 3 tablespoons vegetable oil
- ¼ cup all-purpose flour
- 2 medium onions, chopped
- 1 cup chopped celery
- 1 large green bell pepper, chopped
- 2 cloves garlic, minced
- 3 cups chicken broth
- 1 can (16 ounces) whole tomatoes in juice, undrained
- 1 package (10 ounces) frozen sliced okra
- 1 bay leaf
- 1 teaspoon TABASCO® pepper sauce
- ¾ pound shredded cooked chicken
- ½ pound raw shrimp, peeled, deveined
- Hot cooked rice

Heat oil in large saucepan or Dutch oven. Add flour and cook over low heat until mixture turns dark brown and develops a nutty aroma; stir frequently. Add onions, celery, bell pepper and garlic; cook 5 minutes or until vegetables are tender. Gradually add broth. Stir in tomatoes with juice, okra, bay leaf and TABASCO sauce; bring to a boil. Add chicken and shrimp; cook 3 to 5 minutes or until shrimp turn pink. Remove bay leaf. Serve with rice.

Makes 6 servings

Red Beans and Rice

SOUTH-OF-THE-BORDER SIZZLERS

Rio Grande Quesadillas

- 2 cups shredded cooked chicken
- 1 package (1.25 ounces) LAWRY'S® Taco Spices & Seasonings
- ¾ cup water
- 1 can (16 ounces) refried beans
- 6 large flour tortillas
- 1½ cups (6 ounces) grated Monterey Jack cheese
- ¼ cup chopped pimiento
- ¼ cup chopped green onions
- ¼ cup chopped fresh cilantro
- Vegetable oil
- Chunky salsa and guacamole (optional)

In medium skillet, combine chicken, Taco Spices & Seasonings and water. Bring to a boil; reduce heat and simmer, uncovered, 15 minutes. Stir in refried beans. On half of each tortilla, spread about ⅓ cup chicken-bean mixture. Layer each with equal portions of cheese, pimiento, onions and cilantro. Fold each tortilla in half. In large skillet, heat small amount of oil; quickly fry folded tortilla on each side until slightly crisp and cheese is melted. Repeat with remaining folded tortillas. Cut each quesadilla in quarters and serve with chunky salsa and guacamole, if desired.

Makes 6 servings

Rio Grande Quesadillas

Grilled Prawns with Salsa Vera Cruz

- 1 can (14½ ounces) DEL MONTE® Mexican Recipe Stewed Tomatoes
- 1 orange, peeled and chopped
- ¼ cup sliced green onions
- ¼ cup chopped cilantro or parsley
- 1 tablespoon olive oil
- 1 to 2 teaspoons minced jalapeño chile
- 1 small clove garlic, crushed
- 1 pound medium shrimp, peeled and deveined
- Hot cooked rice (optional)

Drain tomatoes reserving liquid; chop tomatoes. In medium bowl, combine tomatoes, reserved liquid, orange, onions, cilantro, oil, jalapeño and garlic. Season to taste with salt and pepper, if desired. Thread shrimp on skewers; season with salt and pepper, if desired. Brush grill with oil. Cook shrimp over hot coals about 3 minutes per side or until shrimp just turn opaque pink. Top with salsa. Serve over rice, if desired. *Makes 4 servings*

Prep time: 27 minutes
Cook time: 6 minutes

Rice with Tomato and Jalapeño

- 1 green bell pepper, diced
- ½ cup chopped onion
- 1 jalapeño pepper, chopped
- 1 tablespoon olive oil
- 1 recipe Arroz Blanco (page 54)
- 1 can (14½ ounces) whole tomatoes, drained and chopped
- ⅛ teaspoon dried oregano leaves
- 2 tablespoons snipped cilantro, for garnish

Cook bell pepper, onion, and jalapeño pepper in oil in large skillet over medium-high heat until crisp-tender. Stir in Arroz Blanco, tomatoes, and oregano; cook 5 minutes longer. Garnish with cilantro. *Makes 6 servings*

Microwave Directions: Combine bell pepper, onion, jalapeño pepper, and oil in 2- to 3-quart microproof baking dish. Cook at HIGH (100% power) 3 to 4 minutes. Add Arroz Blanco, tomatoes, and oregano; cover with waxed paper and cook at HIGH (100% power) 3 to 4 minutes, stirring after 2 minutes. Garnish with cilantro.

Tip: To reduce the heat level of jalapeño pepper, scrape and discard seeds and membranes before chopping.

Favorite recipe from **USA Rice Council**

Grilled Prawns with Salsa Vera Cruz

Green Enchiladas with Chicken

- 1 pound fresh tomatillos *or* 2 cans (13 ounces each) tomatillos, drained
- 1 can (7 ounces) diced green chilies, undrained
- 2 tablespoons vegetable oil
- 1 medium onion, finely chopped
- 1 clove garlic, minced
- 1 can (14½ ounces) chicken broth
- Vegetable oil for frying
- 12 (6- to 7-inch) corn tortillas
- 3 cups shredded cooked chicken
- 2½ cups (10 ounces) shredded Monterey Jack cheese, divided
- 1 cup (½ pint) sour cream
- 4 green onions with tops, thinly sliced
- Cilantro sprigs, for garnish

Preheat oven to 350°F. If using fresh tomatillos, remove husks; wash thoroughly. Place tomatillos in 2-quart pan; add ½ inch water. Bring to a boil. Cover; reduce heat and simmer 10 minutes or until tender. Drain. Add tomatillos and chilies to food processor or blender. Process until smooth. Heat 2 tablespoons oil in large skillet over medium heat. Add onion and garlic; cook until onion is tender. Stir in tomatillo mixture and chicken broth. Simmer, uncovered, until sauce has reduced to about 2½ cups and is consistency of canned tomato sauce.

Heat ½ inch oil in 7- to 8-inch skillet over medium-high heat. Place 1 tortilla in hot oil; cook 2 seconds on each side or just until limp. Drain briefly on paper towels, then dip softened tortilla into tomatillo sauce. Transfer sauced tortilla to a plate. Place about ¼ cup chicken and 2 tablespoons cheese across center of tortilla; roll to enclose. Place enchilada, seam side down, in 15×10-inch baking pan. Repeat until all tortillas are filled. Spoon remaining sauce over enchiladas, making sure all ends are moistened; reserve remaining cheese. Cover. Bake 20 to 30 minutes or until hot in center. Uncover and top with reserved cheese. Continue baking, uncovered, 10 minutes or until cheese is melted. Spoon sour cream down center of enchiladas; sprinkle with onions. Garnish with cilantro.

Makes 6 servings

Green Enchiladas with Chicken

Chicken with Rice Burritos

Chicken with Rice Burritos

2½ cups shredded cooked chicken
1 package (1.25 ounces) LAWRY'S® Taco Spices & Seasonings
3¼ cups water, divided
2 tablespoons vegetable oil
1 cup long-grain rice, uncooked
1 can (8 ounces) tomato sauce
1 teaspoon LAWRY'S® Lemon Pepper Seasoning
1 large tomato, chopped
¼ cup chopped green onions
6 medium flour tortillas, warmed
Grated Cheddar cheese
Salsa and guacamole (optional)

In large deep skillet, combine chicken, Taco Spices & Seasonings and ¾ cup water. Bring to a boil; reduce heat and simmer, uncovered, 10 minutes. Remove chicken mixture from skillet and set aside. In same skillet, heat oil. Add rice; cook and stir until golden. Add remaining 2½ cups water, tomato sauce and Lemon Pepper Seasoning. Bring to a boil; reduce heat, cover and simmer 20 minutes. Stir in chicken mixture, tomato and onions; blend well. Heat 5 minutes. Place a heaping ½ cup filling in center of each warm tortilla. Fold in sides and roll to enclose filling. Place burritos, seam sides down, on ungreased baking sheet. Sprinkle with cheese. Heat in 350°F oven 5 minutes to melt cheese. Garnish with salsa and guacamole, if desired. *Makes 8 servings*

Green Rice

2 Anaheim chiles
1 jalapeño pepper
1 tablespoon margarine or olive oil
¼ cup sliced green onions
¼ cup snipped cilantro
1 recipe Arroz Blanco (page 54)
¼ teaspoon dried oregano leaves

Chop chiles and jalapeño pepper in food processor until minced but not liquified. Melt margarine in large skillet over low heat. Add chiles mixture; cook 1 minute over medium heat. Stir in onions and cilantro; cook 15 to 30 seconds. Add Arroz Blanco and oregano; heat.
Makes 6 servings

Favorite recipe from **USA Rice Council**

SOUTH-OF-THE-BORDER SIZZLERS 49

Guacamole

- 2 large avocados, pitted and peeled
- ¼ cup finely chopped tomato
- 2 tablespoons lime juice or lemon juice
- 2 tablespoons grated onion
- ½ teaspoon salt
- ¼ teaspoon hot pepper sauce
  Ground black pepper to taste
  Additional chopped tomato (optional)

Place avocados in medium bowl; mash coarsely with fork. Stir in tomato, lime juice, onion, salt and pepper sauce; mix well. Add black pepper. Spoon into serving container. Serve immediately or cover and refrigerate up to 2 hours. Garnish with additional chopped tomato, if desired.

Makes 2 cups

Classic Salsa

- 4 medium tomatoes
- 1 small onion, finely chopped
- 2 to 3 jalapeño peppers or serrano chilies, seeded and minced
- ¼ cup chopped fresh cilantro
- 1 small clove garlic, minced
- 2 tablespoons lime juice
  Salt and ground black pepper to taste

Cut tomatoes in half; remove seeds. Coarsely chop tomatoes. Combine tomatoes, onion, jalapeño peppers, cilantro, garlic and lime juice in medium bowl. Add salt and black pepper. Cover; refrigerate 1 hour or up to 3 days for flavors to blend.

Makes about 2½ cups

Tomatillo Salsa

- 1 pound fresh tomatillos (about 12 large) *or* 1 can (13 ounces) tomatillos
- ½ cup finely chopped red onion
- ¼ cup coarsely chopped fresh cilantro
- 2 jalapeño peppers or serrano chilies, seeded and minced
- 1 tablespoon lime juice
- 1 teaspoon olive oil
- ½ teaspoon salt

If using fresh tomatillos, remove papery husks; wash and finely chop. If using canned tomatillos, drain; coarsely chop.

Combine all ingredients in medium bowl. Cover and refrigerate 1 hour or up to 3 days for flavors to blend.

Makes about 1½ cups

Clockwise from left: Classic Salsa, Guacamole and Tomatillo Salsa

Tacos Picadillos

- ¾ pound ground pork
- 1 medium onion, chopped
- ½ teaspoon ground cinnamon
- ½ teaspoon ground cumin
- 1 can (14½ ounces) DEL MONTE® Mexican Recipe Stewed Tomatoes
- ⅓ cup DEL MONTE® Seedless Raisins
- ⅓ cup toasted chopped almonds
- 6 flour tortillas
- Lettuce, cilantro and sour cream (optional)

In large skillet, brown meat with onion and spices over medium-high heat. Season to taste with salt and pepper, if desired. Stir in tomatoes and raisins. Cover and cook 10 minutes. Remove cover; cook over medium-high heat 5 minutes or until thickened, stirring occasionally. Just before serving, stir in almonds. Fill tortillas with meat mixture; roll to enclose. Garnish with lettuce, cilantro and sour cream, if desired. Serve immediately.

Makes 6 servings

Prep time: 5 minutes
Cook time: 25 minutes

Helpful Hint: If ground pork is not available, boneless pork may be purchased and ground in food processor. Cut pork into 1-inch cubes before processing.

Chilies Rellenos en Casserole

- 3 eggs, separated
- ¾ cup milk
- ¾ cup all-purpose flour
- ½ teaspoon salt
- 1 tablespoon butter or margarine
- ½ cup chopped onion
- 2 cans (7 ounces each) whole green chilies, drained
- 8 ounces Monterey Jack cheese, cut into 8 slices
- Condiments: Sour cream, sliced green onions, pitted ripe olive slices, guacamole, salsa

Preheat oven to 350°F. Add egg yolks, milk, flour and salt to food processor or blender. Process until smooth. Pour into bowl and let stand. Melt butter in small skillet over medium heat. Add onion; cook until tender. Pat chilies dry with paper towels; slit lengthwise and carefully remove seeds. Place 1 slice cheese and 1 tablespoon onion in each chili. Place chilies in single layer in 13×9-inch baking dish.

Beat egg whites until soft peaks form; fold into yolk mixture. Pour over chilies in baking dish. Bake 20 to 25 minutes or until topping is puffed and knife inserted in center comes out clean. Broil 4 inches below heat 30 seconds or until topping is golden brown. Serve with condiments.

Makes 4 servings

Taco Picadillos

Black Bean Garnacha

Black Bean Garnachas

- 1 can (14½ ounces) DEL MONTE® Mexican Recipe Stewed Tomatoes
- 1 can (15 ounces) black or pinto beans, drained
- 2 cloves garlic, minced
- 1 to 2 teaspoons minced jalapeño chiles (optional)
- ½ teaspoon ground cumin
- 1 cup cubed grilled chicken
- 4 flour tortillas
- ½ cup shredded sharp Cheddar cheese
- Shredded lettuce and diced avocado (optional)

Drain tomatoes reserving liquid; chop tomatoes. In large skillet, combine tomatoes, reserved liquid, beans, garlic, jalapeño and cumin. Cook over medium-high heat, 5 to 7 minutes or until thickened, stirring occasionally. Season with salt and pepper, if desired. Add chicken. Arrange tortillas in a single layer on grill over medium coals. Spread about ¾ cup chicken mixture over each tortilla. Top with cheese. Cook about 3 minutes or until bottom of tortilla browns and cheese melts. Garnish with shredded lettuce and diced avocado, if desired.

Makes 4 servings

Prep time: 5 minutes
Cook time: 10 minutes

Arroz Blanco

- 1 tablespoon margarine
- ½ cup chopped onion
- 2 cloves garlic, minced
- 1 cup uncooked rice*
- 2 cups chicken broth

*Recipe based on regular-milled long-grain white rice.

Melt margarine in 2- to 3-quart saucepan over medium heat. Add onion and garlic; cook until onion is tender. Add rice and broth. Bring to a boil; stir. Reduce heat; cover and simmer 15 minutes or until rice is tender and liquid is absorbed. Fluff with fork. *Makes 6 servings*

Favorite recipe from **USA Rice Council**

Tequila-Lime Prawns

- 1 pound medium raw shrimp, shelled and deveined
- 3 tablespoons butter or margarine
- 1 tablespoon olive oil
- 2 large cloves garlic, minced
- 2 tablespoons tequila
- 1 tablespoon lime juice
- ¼ teaspoon salt
- ¼ teaspoon crushed red pepper flakes
- 3 tablespoons coarsely chopped fresh cilantro
- Hot cooked rice (optional)
- Lime wedges for garnish

Pat shrimp dry with paper towels. Heat butter and oil in large skillet over medium heat. When butter is melted, add garlic; cook 30 seconds. Add shrimp; cook 2 minutes, stirring occasionally. Stir in tequila, lime juice, salt and red pepper flakes. Cook 2 minutes or until most of liquid evaporates and shrimp are pink and glazed. Add cilantro; cook 10 seconds. Serve over hot cooked rice, if desired. Garnish with lime wedges.
Makes 3 or 4 servings

Jalapeño Pork & Peaches

- 1 can (16 ounces) peach halves in syrup
- 1½ teaspoons white wine vinegar
- 1¼ teaspoons minced jalapeño pepper
- 4 thin lean pork chops
- ¼ cup seasoned dry bread crumbs
- 1½ teaspoons LAWRY'S® Seasoned Salt
- 1¼ teaspoons LAWRY'S® Garlic Powder with Parsley
- 1 tablespoon vegetable oil
- 1 teaspoon cornstarch
- ½ teaspoon sugar

Drain peaches; reserve ½ cup syrup. Quarter peaches; set aside. In small bowl, combine reserved ½ cup syrup, vinegar and jalapeño pepper. Place pork chops and syrup mixture in resealable plastic bag. Marinate pork chops in refrigerator 30 minutes. In shallow dish, combine bread crumbs, Seasoned Salt and Garlic Powder with Parsley. Remove pork chops from bag, reserving marinade. Dredge pork chops in crumb mixture. In large skillet, heat oil and brown pork chops 4 to 5 minutes on each side or until golden. In small saucepan, combine reserved marinade, cornstarch and sugar. Bring to a boil; reduce heat and simmer 1 minute. Stir in peaches; heat through. Serve sauce over pork chops.
Makes 4 servings

Jalapeño Pork & Peaches

Mexican Flank Steak with Mock Tamales

- 1½ pounds beef flank steak
- ⅓ cup fresh lemon juice
- ⅓ cup extra virgin olive oil
- 6 tablespoons minced jalapeño peppers
- 1 tablespoon minced fresh cilantro
- 1 teaspoon salt
- 1 teaspoon freshly ground black pepper
- Linda's Sassy Salsa (recipe follows)
- Mock Tamales (recipe follows)
- Lemon slices, jalapeño peppers and cilantro sprigs, for garnish

Place beef flank steak in shallow dish. Combine lemon juice, oil, jalapeño peppers, cilantro, salt and black pepper; pour over steak, turning to coat. Cover; refrigerate 6 to 8 hours or overnight. Meanwhile, prepare Linda's Sassy Salsa and Mock Tamales.

Remove steak from marinade; reserve marinade. Place steak on grid over medium-hot coals. Place Mock Tamales around outer edge of grid. Grill steak 12 to 15 minutes to desired doneness (rare or medium), turning once and basting occasionally with marinade. Turn tamales halfway through cooking time. Place steak and tamales on serving platter. Spoon ¼ cup salsa over tamales. Garnish platter with lemon slices, whole jalapeño peppers and cilantro sprigs. Carve steak across grain into thin slices and serve with remaining salsa.

Makes 6 servings

Linda's Sassy Salsa

- 2 tomatillos, hulls and tough skins removed
- 3 large cloves garlic, peeled
- 2 plum tomatoes, minced
- 3 plum tomatoes, coarsely chopped
- 3 jalapeño peppers, thinly sliced
- ¼ cup coarsely chopped fresh cilantro
- 1 tablespoon fresh lemon juice
- 1 teaspoon freshly ground black pepper

Process tomatillos and garlic in food processor or blender until pulverized. Combine tomatillo mixture, tomatoes, jalapeño peppers, cilantro, lemon juice and black pepper. Refrigerate, covered, 1 hour or overnight to blend flavors.

Makes 2 cups

Mock Tamales

- 1 cup (4 ounces) shredded sharp Cheddar cheese
- 1 cup (4 ounces) shredded Muenster cheese
- 2 tablespoons minced green onions and tops
- 6 (7-inch) flour tortillas

Combine cheeses and onions. Place equal portion of cheese mixture in center of each tortilla. Fold bottom side of each tortilla over filling. Fold two sides over filling; fold top side over filling, envelope fashion. Wrap each tamale in 12×8-inch piece of foil, twisting each end.

Makes 6 servings

Favorite recipe from **National Cattlemen's Beef Association**

Mexican Flank Steak with Mock Tamale

Mexicali Appetizer Meatballs

- ⅔ cup A.1.® Steak Sauce
- ⅔ cup mild, medium or hot thick and chunky salsa
- 1½ pounds ground beef
- 1 egg
- ½ cup plain dry bread crumbs

In small bowl, blend steak sauce and salsa. In separate small bowl, combine beef, egg, bread crumbs and ⅓ cup sauce mixture; shape into 32 (1¼-inch) meatballs. Arrange meatballs in single layer in shallow baking pan. Bake at 425°F for 12 to 15 minutes or until meatballs are cooked through. Serve hot meatballs with remaining sauce mixture as a dip.

Makes 32 (1¼-inch) meatballs

Mexicali Appetizer Meatballs

Sonora Shrimp

- 2 tablespoons IMPERIAL® Margarine
- 1 medium green bell pepper, coarsely chopped
- ½ cup chopped onion
- ½ cup chopped celery
- 1 can (14½ ounces) whole peeled tomatoes, undrained and cut up
- ½ cup dry white wine
- ½ teaspoon LAWRY'S® Seasoned Salt
- ½ teaspoon LAWRY'S® Seasoned Pepper
- ¼ teaspoon LAWRY'S® Garlic Powder with Parsley
- ¼ teaspoon dried thyme leaves, crushed
- 1 pound raw medium shrimp, peeled and deveined
- 1 can (2¼ ounces) sliced pitted ripe olives, drained
- Hot cooked rice (optional)

In large skillet, melt margarine; cook and stir bell pepper, onion and celery 5 minutes or until soft. Add remaining ingredients except shrimp and olives; blend well. Bring to a boil; reduce heat and simmer, uncovered, 15 minutes, stirring occasionally. Add shrimp and olives; cook 10 minutes or until shrimp turn pink. Serve over rice, if desired.

Makes 4 to 6 servings

Chili Roasted Turkey Breast

Chili Roasted Turkey Breast

- 1 envelope LIPTON® Recipe Secrets® Onion Soup Mix*
- ¼ cup vegetable oil
- 1½ teaspoons chili powder
- 1½ teaspoons fresh lime juice
- ½ teaspoon LAWRY'S® Garlic Powder with Parsley
- ½ teaspoon ground cumin
- ¼ teaspoon dried oregano leaves
- 1 (5-pound) turkey breast (with bone)

*Also terrific with Lipton® Recipe Secrets® Onion-Mushroom, Beefy Mushroom or Beefy Onion Soup Mix.

Preheat oven to 350°F. In small bowl, blend all ingredients except turkey; let stand 5 minutes. In large roasting pan, place turkey, breast side up. Insert meat thermometer into thickest part of breast, away from bone. Brush soup mixture onto turkey; tent with foil. Roast 1 hour, basting once. Remove foil and continue roasting 1 hour or until meat thermometer reaches 175°F. Let stand, tented with aluminum foil, 10 minutes.

Makes about 6 servings

SOUTH-OF-THE-BORDER SIZZLERS

Deluxe Fajita Nachos

2½ cups shredded, cooked chicken
1 package (1.27 ounces) LAWRY'S® Spices & Seasonings for Fajitas
⅓ cup water
8 ounces tortilla chips
1¼ cups (5 ounces) grated Cheddar cheese
1 cup (4 ounces) grated Monterey Jack cheese
1 large tomato, chopped
1 can (2¼ ounces) sliced ripe olives, drained
¼ cup sliced green onions
Salsa

In medium skillet, combine chicken, Spices & Seasonings for Fajitas and water; blend well. Bring to a boil; reduce heat and simmer 3 minutes. In large shallow ovenproof platter, arrange chips. Top with chicken and cheeses. Place under broiler to melt cheese. Top with tomato, olives, onions and desired amount of salsa.

Makes 4 appetizer or 2 main dish servings

Hint: For a spicier version, add sliced jalapeños.

Spicy Sausage Burritos

8 ounces fresh chorizo sausage or hot-seasoned fresh pork sausage
1 medium potato, peeled and diced
¼ cup chopped onion
4 eggs, beaten
4 flour tortillas, warmed (7- to 8-inch diameter)
4 leaf lettuce leaves
¼ cup (4 ounces) shredded Monterey Jack cheese
1 tomato, chopped
1 avocado, chopped

Remove chorizo sausage from casing. Cook sausage, potato and onion in large skillet over medium-low heat 12 to 15 minutes, breaking sausage into pieces. Pour off drippings. Pour eggs over sausage mixture; cook over medium heat 2 to 3 minutes or until eggs are cooked, stirring frequently. Line each tortilla with lettuce leaf. Place equal amount of sausage mixture in each tortilla; top with equal amount of cheese. Fold bottom side of tortilla over filling. Fold each side of tortilla toward center, overlapping to form pocket. Top with tomato and avocado. Serve immediately.

Makes 4 servings

Preparation time: 15 minutes
Cooking time: 14 to 18 minutes

Favorite recipe from **National Cattlemen's Beef Association**

Deluxe Fajita Nachos

HOT OFF THE GRILL

Beef with Dry Spice Rub

- 3 tablespoons firmly packed brown sugar
- 1 tablespoon black peppercorns
- 1 tablespoon yellow mustard seeds
- 1 tablespoon whole coriander seeds
- 4 cloves garlic
- 1½ to 2 pounds beef top round steak or London Broil (about 1½ inches thick)
- Vegetable or olive oil
- Salt

Place brown sugar, peppercorns, mustard seeds, coriander seeds and garlic in blender or food processor; process until seeds and garlic are crushed. Rub beef with oil, then pat on spice mixture. Season generously with salt.

Oil hot grid to help prevent sticking. Grill beef, on covered grill, over medium-low KINGSFORD® briquets, 16 to 20 minutes for medium doneness, turning once. Let stand 5 minutes before slicing. Cut across grain into thin, diagonal slices.
Makes 6 servings

Beef with Dry Spice Rub

Greek Grilled Chicken

Grilled Greek Chicken

- 1 cup MIRACLE WHIP® Salad Dressing
- ½ cup chopped fresh parsley
- ¼ cup dry white wine or chicken broth
- 1 lemon, sliced and halved
- 2 tablespoons dried oregano leaves, crushed
- 1 tablespoon each: garlic powder, pepper
- 2 (2½- to 3-pound) broiler-fryers, cut up

• Mix together all ingredients except chicken until well blended. Pour over chicken. Cover; marinate in refrigerator at least 20 minutes. Drain marinade; discard.

• Place chicken on grill over medium-hot coals (coals will have slight glow). Grill, covered, 20 to 25 minutes on each side or until tender.

Makes 8 servings

Lip Smackin' Sassy Drummettes

- 32 chicken drummettes
- 1 (18-ounce) jar HUNT'S® All Natural Hot & Spicy Barbecue Sauce
- 1 tablespoon cider vinegar
- 1 teaspoon Worcestershire sauce
- ⅛ teaspoon garlic powder

Preheat oven to 425°F. Line 2 baking sheets with foil; place drummettes in single layer. Bake 35 to 40 minutes; drain. While drummettes are baking, in medium bowl, combine *remaining* ingredients. Place cooked drummettes in bowl and gently spoon sauce over to coat. Return coated drummettes to foil-lined baking sheets; reserve *remaining* sauce. Bake at 375°F for 30 minutes, brushing drummettes with *remaining* sauce halfway through baking.

Makes 32 drummettes

Hot and Spicy Spareribs

- 1 rack pork spareribs, 3 pounds
- 2 tablespoons butter or margarine
- 1 medium onion, finely chopped
- 2 cloves garlic, minced
- 1 can (15 ounces) tomato sauce
- ⅔ cup cider vinegar
- ⅔ cup firmly packed brown sugar
- 2 tablespoons chili powder
- 1 tablespoon prepared mustard
- ½ teaspoon pepper

Melt butter in large skillet over low heat. Add onion and garlic; cook and stir until tender. Add remaining ingredients, except ribs, and bring to a boil. Reduce heat and simmer 20 minutes, stirring occasionally.

Place large piece of aluminum foil over coals to catch drippings. Baste meaty side of ribs with sauce. Place ribs on grill, meaty side down, about 6 inches above low coals; baste top side. Cover. Cook about 20 minutes; turn ribs and baste. Cook 45 minutes more or until done, basting every 10 to 15 minutes with sauce. *Makes 3 servings*

Favorite recipe from **National Pork Producers Council**

Grilled Mexican-Style Burgers

- 1 pound ground beef
- 2 teaspoons instant minced onion
- ¾ teaspoon *each* dried oregano leaves, ground cumin and salt
- ¼ teaspoon pepper
- 1 small tomato, cut into 8 thin slices
- 4 taco shells or flour tortillas
- 1 cup shredded lettuce
- ¼ cup salsa

Combine ground beef, onion, oregano, cumin, salt and pepper, mixing lightly but thoroughly. Divide beef mixture into 4 equal portions; form each into an oval-shaped patty (6×2½ inches). Grill patties on grid over medium coals, turning once. Grill 10 minutes for rare; 12 minutes for medium. To assemble, arrange 2 tomato slices and 1 grilled burger in each taco shell. Top each with ¼ cup lettuce and 1 tablespoon salsa. *Makes 4 servings*

Favorite recipe from **National Cattlemen's Beef Association**

Hot and Spicy Spareribs

Hot, Spicy, Tangy, Sticky Chicken

- 1 chicken (3½ to 4 pounds), cut up
- 1 cup cider vinegar
- 1 tablespoon Worcestershire sauce
- 1 tablespoon chili powder
- 1 teaspoon salt
- 1 teaspoon black pepper
- 1 teaspoon hot pepper sauce
- ¾ cup K.C. MASTERPIECE® Barbecue Sauce

Place chicken in shallow glass dish or large heavy plastic bag. Combine vinegar, Worcestershire sauce, chili powder, salt, pepper and hot pepper sauce in small bowl; pour over chicken pieces. Cover dish or close bag. Marinate in refrigerator at least 4 hours, turning several times.

Oil hot grid to help prevent sticking. Place dark meat pieces on grill 10 minutes before white meat pieces (dark meat takes longer to cook). Grill chicken, on covered grill, over medium KINGSFORD® briquets, 30 to 45 minutes, turning once or twice. Turn and baste with K.C. Masterpiece® Barbecue Sauce during the last 10 minutes of cooking. Chicken is done when meat is no longer pink by bone. Remove chicken from grill; baste with sauce.

Makes 4 servings

Grilled Fish with Chili-Corn Salsa

- 1 cup cooked whole kernel corn
- 1 large tomato, seeded and diced
- ¼ cup thinly sliced green onions with tops
- ¼ cup canned diced green chilies
- 1 tablespoon coarsely chopped cilantro
- ⅛ teaspoon ground cumin
- 1 tablespoon lime juice
- 4 teaspoons olive oil, divided
- Salt
- Pepper
- 1½ pounds firm-textured fish steaks or fillets, such as salmon, halibut, sea bass or swordfish, each 1 inch thick
- Cilantro sprigs for garnish

Combine corn, tomato, onions, chilies, cilantro, cumin, lime juice and 2 teaspoons oil in small bowl; mix well. Add salt and pepper to taste. Let stand at room temperature 30 minutes for flavors to blend. Brush fish with remaining 2 teaspoons oil; season with salt and pepper. Preheat charcoal grill and grease grid. Place fish on grill 4 to 6 inches above solid bed of coals (coals should be evenly covered with grey ashes). Cook, turning once, 4 to 5 minutes on each side or until fish turns opaque and just begins to flake when tested with fork. Serve with salsa. Garnish with cilantro sprigs.

Makes 4 servings

Hot, Spicy, Tangy, Sticky Chicken

Guadalajara Beef

- 1 bottle (12 ounces) Mexican dark beer*
- ¼ cup soy sauce
- 2 cloves garlic, minced
- 1 teaspoon ground cumin
- 1 teaspoon chili powder
- 1 teaspoon hot pepper sauce
- 4 beef bottom sirloin steaks or boneless strip steaks (4 to 6 ounces *each*)
- Salt and black pepper
- Red, green and yellow bell peppers, cut lengthwise into quarters, seeded (optional)
- Salsa (recipe follows)
- Flour tortillas (optional)
- Lime wedges

*Substitute any beer for Mexican dark beer.

Combine beer, soy sauce, garlic, cumin, chili powder and hot pepper sauce in a large shallow glass dish or large heavy plastic bag. Add beef; cover dish or close bag. Marinate in refrigerator up to 12 hours, turning beef several times. Remove beef from marinade; discard marinade. Season with salt and pepper.

Oil hot grid to help prevent sticking. Grill beef and bell peppers, if desired, on covered grill, over medium KINGSFORD® briquets, 8 to 12 minutes, turning once. Beef should be of medium doneness and peppers should be tender. Serve with Salsa, tortillas, if desired, and lime.
Makes 4 servings

Salsa

- 2 cups coarsely chopped seeded tomatoes
- 2 green onions with tops, sliced
- 1 clove garlic, minced
- 1 to 2 teaspoons minced seeded jalapeño or serrano chili pepper, fresh or canned
- 1 tablespoon olive or vegetable oil
- 2 to 3 teaspoons lime juice
- 8 to 10 sprigs fresh cilantro, minced (optional)
- ½ teaspoon salt or to taste
- ½ teaspoon sugar or to taste
- ¼ teaspoon black pepper

Combine tomatoes, green onions, garlic, chili pepper, oil and lime juice in a medium bowl. Stir in cilantro, if desired. Season with salt, sugar and black pepper. Adjust seasonings to taste, adding lime juice or chili pepper, if desired.
Makes about 2 cups

Guadalajara Beef

Texas Barbecue Beef Brisket

Texas Barbecue Beef Brisket

- 1 boneless beef brisket (6 to 8 pounds)
- 2 teaspoons paprika
- 1 teaspoon freshly ground black pepper, divided
- 1 tablespoon butter or margarine
- 1 medium onion, grated
- 1½ cups ketchup
- 1 tablespoon fresh lemon juice
- 1 tablespoon Worcestershire sauce
- 1 teaspoon hot pepper sauce
  Jalapeño peppers, lemon and lime slices (optional)

Trim fat on beef brisket. Combine paprika and ½ teaspoon black pepper; rub evenly over brisket. Place brisket, fat side down, in 11½×9-inch disposable foil pan. Add 1 cup water. Cover pan tightly with aluminum foil. Place in center of grid over very low coals (use single layer of coals with space in between each); cover. Cook 5 hours, turning brisket over every 1½ hours; use baster to remove fat from pan as it accumulates. Add ½ cup water, if necessary, to pan during cooking. Add just enough briquets during cooking to keep coals at a very low temperature. Remove brisket from pan; place on grid, fat side down, directly over very low coals. Reserve pan drippings. Cover; continue cooking 30 minutes.

Meanwhile, skim fat from pan drippings; reserve 1 cup drippings. Melt butter in medium saucepan over medium heat. Add onion; cook until crisp-tender. Add reserved pan drippings, remaining ½ teaspoon pepper, ketchup, lemon juice, Worcestershire sauce and hot pepper sauce; simmer 15 minutes. Carve brisket into thin slices across grain; serve with sauce. Garnish with jalapeño peppers, lemon and lime slices. *Makes 18 to 24 servings*

Note: For smoky flavor, soak oak, pecan, mesquite or hickory chips in water 30 minutes and add to very low coals.

Favorite recipe from **National Cattlemen's Beef Association**

Chicken Ribbons Satay

- ½ cup creamy peanut butter
- ½ cup water
- ¼ cup soy sauce
- 4 cloves garlic, pressed
- 3 tablespoons lemon juice
- 2 tablespoons firmly packed brown sugar
- ¾ teaspoon ground ginger
- ½ teaspoon crushed red pepper flakes
- 4 boneless skinless chicken breast halves
- Sliced green onion tops for garnish

Combine peanut butter, water, soy sauce, garlic, lemon juice, brown sugar, ginger and red pepper flakes in small saucepan. Cook over medium heat 1 minute or until smooth; cool. Remove garlic from sauce; discard. Reserve half the sauce for dipping. Cut chicken lengthwise into 1-inch-wide strips. Thread onto 8 metal or bamboo skewers. (Soak bamboo skewers in water at least 20 minutes to keep them from burning.)

Oil hot grid to help prevent sticking. Grill chicken, on covered grill, over medium-hot KINGSFORD® briquets, 6 to 8 minutes until chicken is cooked through, turning once. Baste with sauce once or twice during cooking. Serve with reserved sauce garnished with sliced green onion tops. *Makes 4 servings*

Pepper Stuffed Flank Steaks

- 2 beef flank steaks (1 pound *each*)
- ¼ teaspoon garlic powder
- ¼ teaspoon black pepper
- 1 green bell pepper, cut into strips
- 1 red bell pepper, cut into strips
- 1 onion, cut into thin slices
- 1 can (15 ounces) tomato sauce
- ½ cup finely chopped onion
- ¼ cup soy sauce
- 1 tablespoon sugar
- 1 teaspoon dry mustard
- 1 teaspoon garlic powder
- ⅛ teaspoon ground red pepper
- ¼ cup vegetable oil

Pound each steak with meat mallet to ¼-inch thickness. Sprinkle steaks with ¼ teaspoon garlic powder and black pepper. Arrange green and red bell pepper strips horizontally on steaks. Cover with onion slices. Starting at narrow end of each steak, roll up jelly-roll fashion; tie with string. Set aside.

Combine tomato sauce, onion, soy sauce, sugar, mustard, 1 teaspoon garlic powder and ground red pepper in large screw-top jar. Shake until well blended. Brush all sides of steaks with oil. Lightly oil grid.

Grill steaks, on covered grill, 4 to 6 inches above hot KINGSFORD® briquets about 30 minutes, turning often, until tender. Brush steaks with tomato-soy sauce mixture during last 10 minutes of grilling.
Makes 6 to 8 servings

Chicken Ribbons Satay

Grilled Swordfish with Tomato Relish

Grilled Swordfish with Tomato Relish

- 1½ pounds tomatoes, peeled and chopped
- 1½ cups chopped onions
- 1 medium red bell pepper, chopped
- 1 cup granulated sugar
- 1 cup HEINZ® Apple Cider Vinegar
- 1 cup HEINZ® 57 Sauce
- ½ cup golden raisins
- 2 teaspoons minced fresh ginger
- 1 clove garlic, crushed
- ½ teaspoon ground coriander
- ¼ teaspoon crushed red pepper
- 2 tablespoons vegetable oil
- 1 tablespoon lemon juice
- ¼ teaspoon lemon pepper seasoning
- ⅛ teaspoon garlic powder
- 6 swordfish steaks, cut ¾ inch thick

For Tomato Relish, combine tomatoes, onions, bell pepper, sugar, vinegar, Heinz® 57 Sauce, raisins, ginger, garlic, coriander and crushed red pepper in large saucepan. Cook, stirring occasionally, over medium-low heat 1 hour or until thick. Cover; refrigerate. (Mixture may be stored in refrigerator for up to 3 weeks.) Let relish stand at room temperature 1 hour before serving.

For swordfish, combine oil, lemon juice, lemon pepper seasoning and garlic powder in small bowl. Brush mixture over swordfish. Spray grid with nonstick cooking spray. Place swordfish on grill over medium-hot coals; grill 5 minutes on each side or until fish flakes easily when tested with fork. Serve swordfish topped with Tomato Relish.

Makes 6 servings

Barbecued Shredded Beef

- 1 (18-ounce) bottle HUNT'S® All Natural Hot & Spicy Barbecue Sauce
- 1 cup water
- 1 cup beer
- 2 cloves garlic, sliced in half
- 1 (2- to 3-pound) flank steak
  Hero or onion rolls

In large Dutch oven, mix together *1 cup* barbecue sauce, water, beer and garlic. Add steak and cook, covered, over low heat 2 hours or until steak is tender. Remove steak and shred into 2-inch strips. Place shredded steak back in pan with *2 cups* cooking liquid and *remaining* barbecue sauce. Stir until well mixed. Simmer 15 to 20 minutes or until most of liquid is absorbed. Serve on hero rolls.

Makes 4 to 6 sandwiches

Spicy Beef Back Ribs

- 1 cup ketchup
- ½ cup water
- 1 medium onion, grated
- 2 tablespoons fresh lemon juice
- 1 teaspoon hot pepper sauce
- ½ to 1 teaspoon crushed red pepper
- 5 pounds beef back ribs, cut into 3 to 4 rib sections

Combine ketchup, water, onion, lemon juice, pepper sauce and red pepper in small saucepan. Bring to a boil; reduce heat. Cook slowly, uncovered, 10 to 12 minutes, stirring occasionally; keep warm. Prepare grill for indirect cooking*. Place beef back ribs, meat side up, on grid centered over drip pan. Cover. Grill ribs 45 to 60 minutes or until tender, turning occasionally. Brush reserved sauce over ribs and continue grilling, covered, 10 minutes.

Makes 5 to 6 servings

*To prepare grill for indirect cooking, arrange equal amount of briquets on each side of grill. Place aluminum foil drip pan in center between coals. Coals are ready when ash-covered, approximately 30 minutes. Make sure coals are burning equally on both sides.

Uncovered Grilling Directions: Place ribs, meat side down, in center of double-thick rectangle of heavy duty aluminum foil. Sprinkle 2 tablespoons water over rib bones. To form packets, bring two opposite sides of aluminum foil together over top of ribs. Fold edges over 3 to 4 times, pressing crease in tightly each time. (Allow some air space.) Flatten aluminum foil at both ends; crease to form triangle and fold each end over several times toward packet, pressing tightly to seal. Place packets on grid over low to medium coals. Grill 2 hours or until tender, turning packets over every ½ hour. Remove ribs from packets and place on grid. Continue grilling 10 to 20 minutes, turning once. Brush sauce over ribs; continue cooking 10 minutes.

Preparation time: 15 minutes
Cooking time: 55 minutes to 1 hour 15 minutes

Favorite recipe from **National Cattlemen's Beef Association**

Spicy Beef Back Ribs

Jalapeño Grilled Chicken

- 1 broiler-fryer chicken, quartered
- 2 tablespoons vegetable oil
- ¼ cup chopped onion
- 1 clove garlic, minced
- 1 cup ketchup
- 2 tablespoons vinegar
- 1 tablespoon brown sugar
- 1 tablespoon minced jalapeño pepper
- ½ teaspoon salt
- ½ teaspoon dry mustard

In saucepan, heat oil to medium temperature. Add onion and garlic; cook, stirring occasionally, about 5 minutes or until onion is tender. Add ketchup, vinegar, brown sugar, jalapeño pepper, salt and mustard. Cook, stirring occasionally, until mixture is blended. Place chicken, skin side up, on prepared grill about 8 inches from heat. Grill, turning every 8 to 10 minutes, about 50 minutes. Brush chicken with sauce; grill, turning and basting with sauce every 5 minutes, about 25 minutes more or until chicken is fork-tender.   *Makes 4 servings*

Favorite recipe from Delmarva Poultry Industry, Inc.

Peppery T-bone Steaks and Chili Corn

- 4 ears fresh sweet corn, in husks
- Cold water
- 1 to 2 cloves garlic, crushed
- ½ teaspoon coarse-grind black pepper
- 2 beef T-bone steaks, cut 1 to 1½ inches thick
- 2 tablespoons butter or margarine
- ½ teaspoon chili powder
- ¼ teaspoon ground cumin

Pull back corn husks from each ear of corn, leaving husks attached to base. Remove corn silk. Fold husks back around corn; tie at end of each ear with string. Soak corn in cold water 3 to 4 hours. Remove corn from water; place on grid over medium coals. Grill 20 minutes, turning often. Meanwhile, combine garlic and pepper; rub evenly into both sides of steaks. Place steaks on grid with corn; grill steaks to desired doneness, turning steaks once and corn often. Grill 1-inch-thick steaks 10 to 14 minutes for rare to medium. Grill 1½-inch-thick steaks 22 to 30 minutes for rare to medium. Remove corn when tender. Meanwhile, melt butter; add chili powder and cumin. Trim excess fat before carving steaks into thick slices. Serve with corn and seasoned butter.   *Makes 4 servings*

Preparation time: 10 minutes
Cooking time: 30 to 50 minutes

Favorite recipe from National Cattlemen's Beef Association

Peppery T-bone Steak and Chili Corn

Fajitas

Fajitas

- ¼ cup lime juice
- ¼ cup tequila
- 2 tablespoons vegetable oil
- 2 cloves garlic, minced
- 1 fresh or canned jalapeño pepper, stemmed, seeded and minced
- 1 tablespoon chopped cilantro
- ¼ teaspoon salt
- ¼ teaspoon ground black pepper
- 1½ pounds beef flank steak
- 2 cans (about 16 ounces each) refried beans
- 8 to 12 flour tortillas, 8-inch diameter

CONDIMENTS
- 2 avocados or guacamole
  Lime juice
  Salsa
  Sour cream

To prepare marinade, combine ¼ cup lime juice, tequila, oil, garlic, jalapeño pepper, cilantro, salt and black pepper in small bowl. Trim any visible fat from meat; place in heavy resealable plastic food storage bag. Pour marinade over meat; seal bag. Refrigerate 8 hours or up to 2 days, turning bag occasionally to distribute marinade.

Preheat charcoal grill and grease grid. Place refried beans in large skillet and heat through; keep warm. Stack and wrap tortillas in foil; place tortillas on side of grill to heat. Remove meat from marinade; reserve marinade. Place meat on grill 4 to 6 inches above solid bed of coals (coals should be medium-glowing). Cook, basting frequently with reserved marinade, 4 minutes on each side for rare or until meat is brown on the outside but still pink when slashed in thickest part. To serve, cut meat across the grain into thin slices; place on warm platter. Peel, pit and chop avocados; sprinkle with lime juice. Place tortillas, refried beans, avocados, salsa and sour cream in separate serving dishes. To serve, wrap meat and condiments in tortilla. *Makes 4 to 6 servings*

Smoke-Cooked Beef Ribs

Wood chunks or chips for smoking
4 to 6 pounds beef back ribs, cut in slabs of 3 to 4 ribs each
Salt and black pepper
1⅓ cups K.C. MASTERPIECE® Barbecue Sauce, divided
Beer at room temperature or hot tap water
Grilled corn-on-the-cob (optional)

Soak 4 wood chunks or several handfuls of wood chips in water; drain. Spread ribs on baking sheet or tray; season with salt and pepper. Brush with half of sauce. Let stand at cool room temperature up to 30 minutes.

Arrange low KINGSFORD® briquets on each side of rectangular metal or foil drip pan. (Since the ribs have been brushed with sauce before cooking, low heat is needed to keep them moist.) Pour in beer to fill pan half full. Add soaked wood (all the chunks; part of the chips) to the fire.

Oil hot grid to help prevent sticking. Place ribs on grid, meaty side up, directly above drip pan. Smoke-cook ribs, on covered grill, about 1 hour, brushing remaining sauce over ribs 2 or 3 times during cooking. If your grill has a thermometer, maintain a cooking temperature between 250°F to 275°F. Add a few more briquets after 30 minutes, or as necessary, to maintain a constant temperature. Add more soaked wood chips every 30 minutes, if necessary. Serve with grilled corn-on-the-cob, if desired.

Makes 4 to 6 servings

Blackened Redfish

½ cup (1 stick) unsalted butter (1 stick), melted *or* ½ cup olive oil, divided
6 (8- to 10-ounce) redfish fillets (or other firm-fleshed fish such as pompano, tilefish, golden tile, red snapper, wall-eyed pike or sac-a-lait) or salmon or tuna steaks (or other freshwater or saltwater fish), at room temperature, cut about ½ inch thick to ¾ inch thick
3 tablespoons plus 2 teaspoons Chef Paul Prudhomme's BLACKENED REDFISH MAGIC®

Heat large cast-iron skillet over very high heat, at least 10 minutes. Meanwhile, pour 2 tablespoons melted butter in each of 6 small ramekins; set aside and keep warm. Reserve remaining butter.

Dip each fillet in reserved melted butter so both sides are coated; sprinkle Blackened Redfish Magic® generously and evenly on both sides of fillets. Place 1 or 2 fillets in skillet and cook, uncovered, over high heat until the bottom is dark brown (but not burned), about 2 minutes (time may vary according to fillet's thickness and heat of skillet). Turn fish over and cook until fish flakes easily when tested with fork, about 2 minutes. Repeat with remaining fillets. Serve each fillet while piping hot.

To serve, place 1 fillet and 1 ramekin of butter on each plate.

Makes 6 servings

Smoke-Cooked Beef Ribs

FIRE ALARM CHILIS

Aztec Chili Salad

- 1 pound ground beef
- 1 package (1.62 ounces) LAWRY'S® Spices & Seasonings for Chili
- ½ cup water
- 1 can (15¼ ounces) kidney beans, undrained
- 1 can (14½ ounces) whole peeled tomatoes, undrained and cut up
- ½ cup dairy sour cream
- 3 tablespoons mayonnaise
- 1 fresh medium tomato, diced
- ¼ cup chopped fresh cilantro
- ½ teaspoon LAWRY'S® Seasoned Pepper
- 1 head lettuce
- 1 red bell pepper, sliced
- ¼ cup sliced green onions
- 1½ cups (6 ounces) grated Cheddar cheese
- ¼ cup sliced ripe olives

In large skillet, brown ground beef until crumbly; drain fat. Stir in Spices & Seasonings for Chili, water, beans and canned tomatoes; blend well. Bring to a boil; reduce heat and simmer, uncovered, 10 minutes. For dressing, in blender or food processor, blend sour cream, mayonnaise, fresh tomato, cilantro and Seasoned Pepper. Refrigerate until chilled. On 6 individual plates, layer lettuce, chili meat, bell pepper, onions, cheese and olives. Drizzle with chilled dressing.

Makes 6 servings

Aztec Chili Salad

Chicken Chili

- 1 pound ground chicken
- 1 medium onion, chopped
- ½ cup chopped green bell pepper
- 1 clove garlic, minced
- 1 can (28 ounces) whole peeled tomatoes, with juice, broken up
- 1 can (16 ounces) kidney beans, undrained
- 1 cup water
- 1 can (6 ounces) tomato paste
- 4 teaspoons chili powder
- 1 teaspoon salt
- 1 teaspoon sugar
- 1 teaspoon ground cumin
- ¼ teaspoon ground red pepper

Spray Dutch oven with nonstick cooking spray; heat over medium-high heat. Add chicken, onion, bell pepper and garlic; cook, stirring, until meat is browned. Add tomatoes with juice, beans, water, tomato paste, chili powder, salt, sugar, cumin and red pepper; stir well. Reduce heat to low; simmer, uncovered, stirring occasionally, about 30 minutes.
Makes 6 servings

Favorite recipe from **Delmarva Poultry Industry, Inc.**

Southern BBQ Chili

- ½ pound lean ground beef
- 1 medium onion, chopped
- 1 clove garlic, minced
- 1 can (14½ ounces) DEL MONTE® Chili Style Chunky Tomatoes
- 1 can (15 ounces) barbecue-style beans
- 1 can (15 ounces) black beans, drained
- 1 can (8¾ ounces) or 1 cup kidney beans, drained
- Low fat sour cream and sliced green onions (optional)

In large saucepan, brown meat, onion and garlic; drain. Add tomatoes and beans. Cover and simmer 15 minutes or until heated through. Garnish with low fat sour cream and green onions, if desired.
Makes 6 servings

Prep time: 5 minutes
Cook time: 20 minutes

Southwestern Chili

- 1 (2½- to 3-pound) beef chuck roast, boned
- 2 tablespoons vegetable oil
- 1 large onion, chopped
- 2 cloves garlic, minced
- 1 can (8 ounces) whole kernel corn
- 1½ pounds fresh tomatoes, coarsely chopped
- ¼ cup KIKKOMAN® Lite Soy Sauce
- 1 tablespoon chili powder
- 1 teaspoon dried oregano, crumbled
- 1 can (4 ounces) diced green chiles

Cut beef into ½-inch cubes; set aside. Heat oil in Dutch oven or large saucepan over high heat. Add onion and garlic; cook and stir until onion is tender. Stir in beef cubes and cook until brown. Meanwhile, reserving liquid, drain corn. Add reserved liquid, tomatoes, lite soy sauce, chili powder and oregano to pan; stir to combine. Cover and simmer 1 hour and 15 minutes. Uncover; simmer 45 minutes longer, or until meat is tender. Stir in corn and chiles and cook until heated through.
Makes 6 to 8 servings

FIRE ALARM CHILIS

Chili Go Rounds

Chili Go Rounds

- 1 cup finely chopped fully-cooked smoked sausage
- 2 tablespoons HEINZ® Chili Sauce
- 1 tablespoon grated Parmesan cheese
- ¼ teaspoon ground cinnamon
- ¼ teaspoon dried thyme leaves, crushed
- 1 package (8 ounces) refrigerated crescent dinner rolls

In small bowl, combine sausage, chili sauce, Parmesan cheese, cinnamon and thyme. Remove half of dough from container; unroll. Place dough between 2 pieces of waxed paper and roll into 13×5×⅛-inch rectangle. Spread ½ of sausage mixture over dough. Roll, jelly-roll fashion, starting at longest side. Cut into ½-inch slices with sharp knife; place cut-side down on baking sheet. Repeat with remaining dough and sausage mixture. Bake in preheated 375°F oven, 12 to 14 minutes or until golden brown.

Makes about 4 dozen appetizers

FIRE ALARM CHILIS

Santa Fe Stew Olé

Santa Fe Stew Olé

1 tablespoon vegetable oil
1½ pounds beef stew meat, cut into bite-size pieces
1 can (28 ounces) stewed tomatoes
2 medium carrots, cut into ¼-inch slices
1 medium onion, coarsely chopped
1 package (1.25 ounces) LAWRY'S® Taco Spices & Seasonings
2 tablespoons diced green chiles
½ teaspoon LAWRY'S® Seasoned Salt
¼ cup water
2 tablespoons all-purpose flour
1 can (15 ounces) pinto beans, drained

In Dutch oven, heat oil; brown stew meat. Add tomatoes, carrots, onion, Taco Spices & Seasonings, green chiles and Seasoned Salt; blend well. Bring to a boil; reduce heat. Cover and simmer 40 minutes. In small bowl, combine water and flour; blend well. Stir into stew mixture. Add pinto beans; simmer an additional 15 minutes.   *Makes 4 servings*

Chilly Day Chili

2 medium onions, chopped
1 green bell pepper, chopped
2 tablespoons vegetable oil
2 pounds lean ground beef
2 to 3 tablespoons chili powder
1 can (16 ounces) whole peeled tomatoes, undrained and cut into bite-size pieces
1 can (15 ounces) tomato sauce
½ cup HEINZ® Tomato Ketchup
1 teaspoon salt
¼ teaspoon black pepper
2 cans (15 ounces each) red kidney beans, partially drained

In large saucepot or Dutch oven, cook and stir onions and bell pepper in oil until crisp-tender. Add beef; cook until beef is browned, stirring occasionally. Drain excess fat. Stir in chili powder; add tomatoes, tomato sauce, ketchup, salt and pepper. Simmer, uncovered, 30 minutes, stirring occasionally. Add kidney beans; simmer, uncovered, an additional 15 minutes.
       Makes 10 servings

FIRE ALARM CHILIS

Chili Burrito Cups

- 1 (2½-pound) boneless beef chuck pot roast
- 1 medium onion, sliced
- ½ teaspoon salt
- ¼ teaspoon black pepper
- 1 large onion, chopped
- 1 tablespoon vegetable oil
- 1 can (about 16 ounces) pinto, kidney or pink beans, drained
- 1 can (14½ to 16 ounces) whole peeled tomatoes, with juice
- 1 can (6 ounces) tomato paste
- 1 can (4 ounces) chopped green chilies
- 1 tablespoon chili powder
- 8 Microwave Tortilla Cups (recipe follows)
  Sour cream and guacamole (optional)

Cut boneless beef chuck pot roast into three to four pieces. Place beef, sliced onion, salt and pepper in Dutch oven. Add water to measure ½ inch up side of pan; cover tightly and cook at low heat on range top or in 300°F oven 2 to 2½ hours or until beef is tender. Cool slightly in juices. Skim off fat. Pour off juices, reserving 1 cup. Shred beef along the grain using two forks; reserve.* In same Dutch oven, cook and stir chopped onion in oil until tender. Add reserved shredded beef, reserved 1 cup juices, beans, tomatoes, tomato paste, chilies and chili powder. Bring to a boil; reduce heat and simmer 1 hour or until thickened, stirring occasionally.

*Shredded beef may be prepared, covered and refrigerated up to one day ahead.

Meanwhile, prepare Microwave Tortilla Cups. Spoon an equal amount of beef mixture into each tortilla cup. Serve with sour cream and guacamole, if desired.
Makes 8 servings

Microwave Tortilla Cups

Gently press four 7- to 8-inch flour tortillas into four 10-ounce custard cups. Microwave at HIGH (100% power) 2 minutes. Rotate and rearrange custard cups; continue cooking at HIGH (100% power) 1 to 2 minutes. Carefully lift tortillas out and cool on wire rack for 5 minutes. Repeat procedure to make eight tortilla cups.

Prep time: 20 minutes
Cook time: 3 hours 10 minutes to 3 hours 40 minutes

Favorite recipe from **National Cattlemen's Beef Association**

Chili Burrito Cups

Spicy Quick and Easy Chili

- 1 pound ground beef
- 1 large clove garlic, minced
- 1 can (17 ounces) DEL MONTE® Whole Kernel Golden Sweet Corn, drained
- 1 can (16 ounces) kidney beans, drained
- 1 can (14½ ounces) DEL MONTE® Chili Style Chunky Tomatoes
- 1 can (4 ounces) diced green chiles
- Green onions (optional)

In large saucepan, brown meat with garlic; drain. Add remaining ingredients. Simmer, uncovered, 10 minutes, stirring occasionally. Garnish with green onions, if desired.
Makes 4 servings

Variation: For a zestier chili serve with hot pepper sauce or cayenne pepper.

Prep & Cook time: 15 minutes

Southwest Chili

- 1 large onion, chopped
- 1 tablespoon olive oil
- 2 large tomatoes, chopped
- 1 can (4 ounces) chopped green chilies, undrained
- 1 tablespoon chili powder
- 1 teaspoon ground cumin
- 1 can (15 ounces) red kidney beans, undrained
- 1 can (15 ounces) Great Northern beans, undrained
- ¼ cup cilantro leaves, chopped (optional)

Cook and stir onion in oil in large saucepan over medium heat until onion is soft. Stir in tomatoes, chilies, chili powder and cumin. Bring to a boil. Add beans with liquid. Reduce heat to low. Cover and simmer 15 minutes, stirring occasionally. Sprinkle individual servings with cilantro, if desired.
Makes 4 servings

Texas Fajita Chili

- 1¼ cups chopped onion
- 1 cup chopped green bell pepper
- 1 tablespoon vegetable oil
- 2 cans (15 ounces each) kidney beans, drained
- 1 pound shredded, cooked pork or beef
- 1 can (14½ ounces) whole peeled tomatoes, with juice, cut up
- 1 cup LAWRY'S® Fajitas Skillet Sauce
- 1 can (7 ounces) whole kernel corn, drained
- ½ cup tomato juice or beer
- 1½ teaspoons chili powder

In large skillet, cook and stir onion and bell pepper in oil 10 minutes or until tender. Stir in kidney beans, shredded meat, tomatoes, Fajitas Skillet Sauce, corn, tomato juice and chili powder. Bring mixture to a boil; reduce heat, cover and simmer 20 minutes.
Makes 6 servings

Spicy Quick and Easy Chili

Arizona Pork Chili

- 1½ pounds boneless pork, cut into ¼-inch cubes
- 1 tablespoon vegetable oil
- 1 onion, coarsely chopped
- 2 cloves garlic, minced
- 1 can (15 ounces) black, pinto or kidney beans, drained
- 1 can (14½ ounces) DEL MONTE® Chili Style Chunky Tomatoes
- 1 can (4 ounces) diced green chiles
- 1 teaspoon ground cumin
  Tortillas and sour cream (optional)

In large skillet, brown meat in oil over medium-high heat. Add onion and garlic; cook until onion is tender. Season with salt and pepper, if desired. Add remaining ingredients. Simmer 10 minutes, stirring occasionally. Serve with tortillas and sour cream, if desired.

Makes 6 servings

Prep time: 10 minutes
Cook time: 25 minutes

Chunky Ancho Chili with Beans

- 5 dried ancho chilies
- 2 cups water
- 2 tablespoons lard or vegetable oil
- 1 large onion, chopped
- 2 cloves garlic, minced
- 1 pound lean boneless beef, cut into 1-inch cubes
- 1 pound lean boneless pork, cut into 1-inch cubes
- 1 to 2 fresh or canned jalapeño peppers, stemmed, seeded and minced
- 1 teaspoon salt
- 1 teaspoon dried oregano, crushed
- 1 teaspoon ground cumin
- ½ cup dry red wine
- 3 cups cooked pinto beans *or* 2 cans (15 ounces each) pinto or kidney beans, drained

Rinse ancho chilies; remove stems, seeds and veins. Place in 2-quart pan with water. Bring to a boil; turn off heat and let stand, covered, 30 minutes or until chilies are soft. Pour chilies with liquid into blender or food processor. Process until smooth; reserve.

Melt lard in 5-quart kettle over medium heat. Add onion and garlic; cook until onion is tender. Add beef and pork; cook, stirring frequently, until meat is lightly colored. Add jalapeño peppers, salt, oregano, cumin, wine and ancho chili purée. Bring to a boil. Cover; reduce heat and simmer 1½ to 2 hours or until meat is very tender. Stir in beans. Simmer, uncovered, 30 minutes or until chili has thickened slightly. Serve in individual bowls.

Makes 8 servings

Arizona Pork Chili

Chili á la Mexico

Chili á la Mexico

- 2 pounds ground beef
- 2 cups finely chopped onions
- 2 cloves garlic, minced
- 1 can (28 ounces) whole peeled tomatoes, undrained, coarsely chopped
- 1 can (6 ounces) tomato paste
- 1½ to 2 tablespoons chili powder
- 1 teaspoon ground cumin
- ¼ teaspoon salt
- ¼ teaspoon ground red pepper (optional)
- ¼ teaspoon ground cloves (optional)
- **Lime wedges and cilantro sprigs, for garnish**

Brown beef in deep 12-inch skillet over medium-high heat 6 to 8 minutes, stirring to separate meat. Reduce heat to medium. Pour off drippings. Add onions and garlic; cook and stir 5 minutes or until onions are softened.

Stir in tomatoes, tomato paste, chili powder, cumin, salt, red pepper and cloves. Bring to a boil over high heat. Reduce heat to low. Cover and simmer 30 minutes, stirring occasionally. Ladle into bowls. Garnish with lime wedges and cilantro. *Makes 6 to 8 servings*

Rick's Good-as-Gold Chili

- ⅓ cup water
- ¼ cup instant minced onion
- 2 teaspoons instant minced garlic
- ½ cup vegetable oil
- 1½ pounds skinless boneless chicken breast chunks
- 1 can (15 ounces) tomato sauce
- ¾ cup beer
- ½ cup chicken broth
- 2 tablespoons chili powder
- 2 teaspoons ground cumin
- 1 teaspoon dried oregano, crushed
- 1 teaspoon soy sauce
- 1 teaspoon Worcestershire sauce
- ¾ teaspoon salt
- ½ teaspoon paprika
- ½ teaspoon ground red pepper
- ¼ teaspoon ground turmeric
- ⅛ teaspoon rubbed sage
- ⅛ teaspoon dried thyme, crushed
- ⅛ teaspoon dry mustard

Combine water, onion and garlic in small bowl; let stand 10 minutes to soften. Heat oil in large skillet over medium-high heat until hot. Brown half the chicken in skillet. Remove with slotted spoon; set aside. Repeat with remaining chicken.

Pour off all but 2 tablespoons oil from skillet; heat oil until hot. Add softened onion and garlic; cook and stir about 5 minutes or until golden. Add remaining ingredients and chicken; mix well. Bring to a boil. Reduce heat and simmer, stirring occasionally, 20 minutes or until sauce thickens slightly.

Makes 4½ cups

Favorite recipe from **American Spice Trade Association**

Southwest Vegetable Chili

- 1 cup coarsely chopped onions
- 1 medium green bell pepper, cut into ½-inch pieces
- 2 cloves garlic, minced
- ½ cup water
- 2 beef bouillon cubes
- 1 tablespoon chili powder
- ½ teaspoon cumin
- ¼ cup HEINZ® Gourmet Wine Vinegar
- 1 can (15 ounces) kidney beans, undrained
- 1 can (14½ ounces) tomatoes, with juice, cut into bite-size pieces
- 1 can (11 ounces) whole kernel corn, drained
- Hot cooked rice

In 3-quart saucepan, combine onions, bell pepper, garlic, water, bouillon, chili powder and cumin; simmer, covered, 5 minutes or until vegetables are tender. Stir in vinegar, beans, tomatoes and corn. Bring mixture to a boil; simmer, uncovered, 30 minutes, stirring occasionally. To serve, spoon vegetable chili into individual bowls and top with rice.

Makes 4 servings

Tex-Mex Chili

- 4 bacon slices, diced
- 2 pounds beef round steak, trimmed and cut into ½-inch cubes
- 1 medium onion, chopped
- 2 cloves garlic, minced
- ¼ cup chili powder
- 1 teaspoon dried oregano, crushed
- 1 teaspoon ground cumin
- 1 teaspoon salt
- ½ to 1 teaspoon ground red pepper
- ½ teaspoon hot pepper sauce
- 4 cups water
- Chopped onion, for garnish

Cook bacon in 5-quart kettle over medium-high heat until crisp. Remove with slotted spoon; drain on paper towels. Add half the steak to bacon drippings in kettle; cook until lightly browned. Remove steak from kettle. Repeat with remaining steak. Reduce heat to medium. Cook medium onion and garlic in pan drippings until onion is tender. Reduce heat to medium. Return steak and bacon to kettle. Add chili powder, oregano, cumin, salt, ground red pepper, hot pepper sauce and water. Bring to a boil. Cover; reduce heat and simmer 1½ hours. Skim fat. Simmer, uncovered, 30 minutes or until steak is very tender and chili has thickened slightly. Serve in individual bowls. Garnish with chopped onion.

Makes 6 servings

Rick's Good-as-Gold Chili

FIRE ALARM CHILIS

Easy Chili con Carne

- ½ medium onion, chopped
- 1 stalk celery, sliced
- 1 teaspoon chili powder
- 1 can (15¼ ounces) kidney beans, drained
- 1 can (14½ ounces) DEL MONTE® Chili Style Chunky Tomatoes
- 1 cup cubed cooked beef
- Hot pepper sauce (optional)

Microwave Directions: In 2-quart microwavable dish, combine onion, celery and chili powder. Add 1 tablespoon water. Cover and microwave on HIGH 3 to 4 minutes. Add remaining ingredients. Cover and microwave on HIGH 6 to 8 minutes or until heated through, stirring halfway through. For a spicier chili, serve with hot pepper sauce, if desired. *Makes 4 servings*

Prep time: 8 minutes
Microwave cook time: 12 minutes

Bunkhouse Chili

- 2 pounds lean beef for stew, cut into ½-inch cubes
- 2 tablespoons vegetable oil
- 1 medium green bell pepper, chopped
- 1 medium onion, chopped
- 1 cup chopped celery
- 2 cloves garlic, minced
- 1 can (16 ounces) whole peeled tomatoes, cut into bite-size pieces
- 1½ cups (12 ounces) beer
- 1 cup HEINZ® Thick and Rich Original Recipe or Old Fashioned Barbecue Sauce
- 1 to 2 tablespoons chili powder
- 1 teaspoon dried oregano leaves, crushed
- 1 teaspoon salt
- ¼ teaspoon black pepper
- 2 cans (15 to 17 ounces each) red kidney or pinto beans, drained
- Shredded Cheddar cheese
- Sliced green onions

In Dutch oven or large saucepan, brown beef, one layer at a time, in oil. Add bell pepper, onion, celery and garlic; cook and stir until crisp-tender. Stir in tomatoes, beer, barbecue sauce, chili powder, oregano, salt and pepper. Cover; simmer 1 hour, stirring occasionally. Add kidney beans; simmer, uncovered, 45 minutes, stirring occasionally. Sprinkle with cheese and onions just before serving.
Makes 6 to 8 servings

Bunkhouse Chili

Hot 'n Spicy Beef Chili

Hot 'n Spicy Beef Chili

- 3 pounds boneless beef round or chuck, cut into ¾-inch pieces
- 3 tablespoon vegetable oil, divided
- ½ cup hot chili powder
- 3 medium onions, chopped
- 4 cloves garlic, crushed
- 1 can (7 to 8 ounces) whole jalapeño peppers, seeded and chopped
- 1 can (28 ounces) peeled whole tomatoes, undrained
- 2 tablespoons packed brown sugar
- 1 tablespoon *each* ground cumin, dried oregano leaves, salt and red wine vinegar
- 3 bay leaves
- 2 cups drained ripe olives, sliced
- 1 tablespoon masa harina*
  Shredded Cheddar cheese

*Masa harina is flour made from the ground corn used to make tortillas. It can be found in Mexican section of most supermarkets.

Brown beef cubes, ½ at a time, in 1½ tablespoons oil in Dutch oven. Stir in chili powder. Remove beef mixture; reserve. Heat remaining 1½ tablespoons oil in same Dutch oven. Add onions, garlic and jalapeño peppers; cook until golden, stirring occasionally. Return beef mixture to pan; add tomatoes with juice. Cook 20 minutes, stirring occasionally. Add brown sugar, cumin, oregano, salt, wine vinegar and bay leaves. Cook slowly, uncovered, 2 hours or until beef is tender; stir often. Add olives and masa harina. Remove bay leaves. Serve with cheese.

Makes about 6 servings

Preparation time: 20 minutes
Cooking time: 2 hours 30 minutes

Favorite recipe from **National Cattlemen's Beef Association**

ACKNOWLEDGMENTS

The publisher would like to thank the companies and organizations listed below for the use of their recipes and photographs in this publication.

American Spice Trade Association
Best Foods, a Division of CPC International Inc.
Chef Paul Prudhomme's Magic Seasoning Blends®
Clear Springs Foods
Delmarva Poultry Industry, Inc.
Del Monte Corporation
Heinz U.S.A.
Hunt Food Co.
Kikkoman International Inc.
The Kingsford Products Company
Kraft Foods, Inc.
Lawry's® Foods, Inc.
Thomas J. Lipton Co.
McIlhenny Company
Nabisco, Inc.
National Cattlemen's Beef Association
National Fisheries Institute
National Pork Producers Council
Reckitt & Colman Inc.
Riviana Foods Inc.
USA Rice Council

INDEX

Appetizers
    Cajun-Style Chicken Nuggets, 34
    Chicken Ribbons Satay, 70
    Chili Go Rounds, 81
    Classic Salsa, 50
    Deluxe Fajita Nachos, 60
    Guacamole, 50
    Linda's Sassy Salsa, 56
    Lip Smackin' Sassy Drummettes, 64
    Mexicali Appetizer Meatballs, 58
    Mock Tamales, 56
    Rio Grande Quesadillas, 44
    Salsa, 68
    Spicy Chicken Wings, 15
    Tomatillo Salsa, 50
Arizona Pork Chili, 86
Arroz Blanco, 54
Aztec Chili Salad, 78

Barbecued Shredded Beef, 72
Bayou Dirty Rice, 35
Bean Threads with Minced Pork, 14
Beef
    Aztec Chili Salad, 78
    Barbecued Shredded Beef, 72
    Beef with Dry Spice Rub, 62
    Bunkhouse Chili, 90
    Cantonese-Style Beef and Peppers, 19
    Chili á la Mexico, 88
    Chili Burrito Cups, 83
    Chilly Day Chili, 82
    Chunky Ancho Chili with Beans, 86
    Easy Chili con Carne, 90
    Fajitas, 75
    Grilled Mexican-Style Burgers, 65
    Guadalajara Beef, 68
    Hot 'n Spicy Beef Chili, 91
    Mexicali Appetizer Meatballs, 58
    Mexican Flank Steak with Mock Tamales, 56
    Pepper Stuffed Flank Steaks, 70
    Peppery T-bone Steaks and Chili Corn, 74
    Santa Fe Stew Olé, 82
    Shanghai Salad, 15
    Smoke-Cooked Beef Ribs, 76
    Southern BBQ Chili, 80
    Southwestern Chili, 80
    Spicy Beef Back Ribs, 73
    Spicy Quick and Easy Chili, 84
    Steak Etouffée, 34
    Texas Barbecue Beef Brisket, 69
    Tex-Mex Chili, 89
Beef with Dry Spice Rub, 62
Black Bean Garnachas, 54
Blackened Redfish, 76
Bunkhouse Chili, 90

Cajun Chicken, 32
Cajun-Style Chicken Nuggets, 34
Cantonese-Style Beef and Peppers, 19
Chicken
    Black Bean Garnachas, 54
    Cajun Chicken, 32
    Cajun-Style Chicken Nuggets, 34
    Chicken, Andouille Smoked Sausage and Tasso Jambalaya, 26
    Chicken Creole, 39
    Chicken Curry Bombay, 6
    Chicken Ribbons Satay, 70
    Chicken Smothered in Roasted Garlic with Sweet Basil Red Gravy, 41
    Chicken with Rice Burritos, 49
    Creole Chicken Jambalaya, 30
    Deluxe Fajita Nachos, 60
    Fiery Chicken with Noodles, 9
    Green Enchiladas with Chicken, 48
    Grilled Greek Chicken, 64
    Hoisin Chicken, 16
    Hot Chicken with Peanuts, 13
    Hot, Spicy, Tangy, Sticky Chicken, 66
    Jalapeño Grilled Chicken, 74
    Kung Pao Chicken, 23
    Lip Smackin' Sassy Drummettes, 64
    Louisiana Shrimp and Chicken Gumbo, 42
    Peanut Chicken, 10
    Rick's Good-as-Gold Chili, 88
    Rio Grande Quesadillas, 44
    Sausage-Chicken Creole, 33
    Spicy Chicken Wings, 15
    Tandoori Chicken, 18
    Thai Chicken Curry, 21
Chicken, Andouille Smoked Sausage and Tasso Jambalaya, 26
Chicken Chili, 80
Chicken Creole, 39
Chicken Curry Bombay, 6
Chicken Ribbons Satay, 70
Chicken Smothered in Roasted Garlic with Sweet Basil Red Gravy, 41
Chicken with Rice Burritos, 49
Chili á la Mexico, 88
Chili Burrito Cups, 83
Chilies Rellenos en Casserole, 52
Chili Go Rounds, 81
Chili Roasted Turkey Breast, 59
Chilly Day Chili, 82
Chunky Ancho Chili with Beans, 86
Classic Salsa, 50
Creole Chicken Jambalaya, 30

Deluxe Fajita Nachos, 60

Easy Chili con Carne, 90
Eggplant Szechuan Style, 11

Fajitas, 75
Fiery Chicken with Noodles, 9
Fish (see **Seafood**)
Flaky Southern Biscuits, 33

Green Enchiladas with Chicken, 48
Green Rice, 49
Grilled Fish with Chili-Corn Salsa, 66
Grilled Greek Chicken, 64
Grilled Lobster with Spicy Sauce, 8
Grilled Mexican-Style Burgers, 65
Grilled Prawns with Salsa Vera Cruz, 46
Grilled Rainbow Trout with Asian Flavors, 14
Grilled Swordfish with Tomato Relish, 72
Guacamole, 50
Guadalajara Beef, 68

Hoisin Chicken, 16
Hot 'n Spicy Beef Chili, 91
Hot and Spicy Barbecued Shrimp, 39
Hot and Spicy Spareribs, 65
Hot Chicken with Peanuts, 13

Jalapeño Grilled Chicken, 74
Jalapeño Pork & Peaches, 55
Jambalaya, 32

Kung Pao Chicken, 23

Linda's Sassy Salsa, 56
Lip Smackin' Sassy Drummettes, 64
Louisiana Barbecue Ribs, 29
Louisiana Pork Chops, 30
Louisiana Shrimp and Chicken Gumbo, 42

Mexicali Appetizer Meatballs, 58
Mexican Flank Steak with Mock Tamales, 56
Microwave Recipes
    Easy Chili con Carne, 90
    Microwave Tortilla Cups, 83
    Spicy Shrimp with Snow Peas, 8
Microwave Tortilla Cups, 83
Mock Tamales, 56
Mongolian Lamb, 10

Okra-Bacon Casserole, 37
Orient Express Stir-Fry Sauce, 8

Peanut Chicken, 10
Pepper Stuffed Flank Steaks, 70
Peppery T-bone Steaks and Chili Corn, 74
Pork
    Arizona Pork Chili, 86
    Bean Threads with Minced Pork, 14
    Chunky Ancho Chili with Beans, 86
    Hot and Spicy Spareribs, 65
    Jalapeño Pork & Peaches, 55
    Louisiana Barbecue Ribs, 29
    Louisiana Pork Chops, 30
    Spicy Grilled Pork Chops, 16
    Spicy-Sweet Pineapple Pork, 21
    Sweet 'n Spicy Ribs, 23
    Tacos Picadillos, 52
    Texas Fajita Chili, 84
    Thai Ribs, 13
    Two-Onion Pork Shreds, 20

Red Beans and Rice, 42
Rice with Tomato and Jalapeño, 46
Rick's Good-as-Gold Chili, 88
Rio Grande Quesadillas, 44

Salsa, 68
Santa Fe Stew Olé, 82
Sausage
    Bayou Dirty Rice, 35
    Chicken, Andouille Smoked Sausage and Tasso Jambalaya, 26
    Chili Go Rounds, 81
    Creole Chicken Jambalaya, 30
    Jambalaya, 32
    Red Beans and Rice, 42
    Sausage-Chicken Creole, 33
    Sausage Ham Jambalaya, 38
    Spicy Sausage Burritos, 60
Seafood
    Blackened Redfish, 76
    Grilled Fish with Chili-Corn Salsa, 66
    Grilled Lobster with Spicy Sauce, 8
    Grilled Prawns with Salsa Vera Cruz, 46
    Grilled Rainbow Trout with Asian Flavors, 14
    Grilled Swordfish with Tomato Relish, 72
    Hot and Spicy Barbecued Shrimp, 39
    Louisiana Shrimp and Chicken Gumbo, 42
    Seafood Gumbo, 24, 37
    Shrimp Creole, 28
    Shrimp Etoufée, 32
    Shrimp Gumbo, 30
    Sonora Shrimp, 58
    Spicy Crab Soup, 35
    Spicy Shrimp with Snow Peas, 8
    Tequila-Lime Prawns, 55
Seafood Gumbo, 24, 37
Shanghai Salad, 15
Shrimp Creole, 28
Shrimp Etoufée, 32
Shrimp Gumbo, 30
Side Dishes
    Arroz Blanco, 54
    Bayou Dirty Rice, 35
    Green Rice, 49
    Rice with Tomato and Jalapeño, 46
Smoke-Cooked Beef Ribs, 76
Sonora Shrimp, 58
Southern BBQ Chili, 80
Southwest Chili, 84
Southwestern Chili, 80
Southwest Vegetable Chili, 89
Spicy Beef Back Ribs, 73
Spicy Chicken Wings, 15
Spicy Crab Soup, 35
Spicy Grilled Pork Chops, 16
Spicy Quick and Easy Chili, 84
Spicy Sausage Burritos, 60
Spicy Shrimp with Snow Peas, 8
Spicy-Sweet Pineapple Pork, 21
Steak Etouffée, 34
Stir-Fries
    Bean Threads with Minced Pork, 14
    Cantonese-Style Beef and Peppers, 19
    Eggplant Szechuan Style, 11
    Hoisin Chicken, 16
    Hot Chicken with Peanuts, 13
    Kung Pao Chicken, 23
    Mongolian Lamb, 10
    Shanghai Salad, 15
    Two-Onion Pork Shreds, 20
Sweet 'n Spicy Ribs, 23

Tacos Picadillos, 52
Tandoori Chicken, 18
Tequila-Lime Prawns, 55
Texas Barbecue Beef Brisket, 69
Texas Fajita Chili, 84
Tex-Mex Chili, 89
Thai Chicken Curry, 21
Thai Ribs, 13
Tomatillo Salsa, 50
Tortillas
    Black Bean Garnachas, 54
    Chicken with Rice Burritos, 49
    Chili Burrito Cups, 83
    Fajitas, 75
    Green Enchiladas with Chicken, 48
    Grilled Mexican-Style Burgers, 65
    Microwave Tortilla Cups, 83
    Mock Tamales, 56
    Rio Grande Quesadillas, 44
    Spicy Sausage Burritos, 60
    Tacos Picadillos, 52
Two-Onion Pork Shreds, 20